大展好書　好書大展
品嘗好書　冠群可期

大展好書　好書大展
品嘗好書　冠群可期

▲作者的少林拳　Shaolin Boxing of the Author

▲武術雜誌上的耿軍
Geng Jun on the Cover of Wushu Magazine

▲英法武術代表團訪問孟州少林武術院
The Wushu Delegation of France and UK is visiting the Meng zhou Shaolin Wushu Institute

▲作者部分弟子參加武打片拍攝
Parts of students of author take part in fliming Acrobatic fighting film

▲作者與恩師素法大師
The Author and his Teacher Grandmaster Sufa

▲作者指導女兒耿瑞濤練功
The Author is coaching his daughter to practise her skill

▲作者與原國家武術協會主席張耀庭
The Author and the former Chairman of the Chinese Wushu
Association Zhang Yaoting

▲作者的少林拳　Shaolin Boxing of the Author

▲武術雜誌封面上的耿軍
Geng Jun on the Cover of Wushu Magazine

▲作者與恩師素法大師
The Author and his Teacher Grandmaster Sufa

▲ 作者率領國外弟子朝拜少林寺　Author leads foreign students to visit Shaolin Temple

▲作者與武僧教頭德揚師兄在捶譜堂
In Chuipu Hall, the author and his senior fellow apprentice
who is also the wushu monk teacher deyang

▲作者與中國政協副主席萬國權
The Author and the vice Chairman of the Chinese People's Political
Consultative Conference （CPPCC）Wan Guoquan

▲作者傳藝國際黑帶功夫總會
The Author is teaching his Wushu skill in International Black Belt Kungfu Federation

▲作者指導兒子耿鵬飛練功
The Author is coaching his son Geng Pengfei to practise his skill

少林傳統功夫漢英對照系列 ⑤

Shaolin Traditional Kungfu Series Books ⑤

七星螳螂拳

Seven-star Mantis Boxing（Plum Blossom Routine）

梅花路

耿　軍
Written by Geng Jun　著
趙會斌
Zhao Huibin

大展出版社有限公司

作者簡介

　　耿軍（法號釋德君），1968 年 11 月出生於河南省孟州市，係少林寺三十一世皈依弟子。中國武術七段、全國十佳武術教練員、中國少林武術研究會副秘書長、焦作市政協十屆常委、濟南軍區特警部隊特邀武功總教練、洛陽師範學院客座教授、英才教育集團董事長。1989 年創辦孟州少林武術院、2001 年創辦英才雙語學校。先後獲得河南省優秀青年新聞人物、全國優秀武術教育家等榮譽稱號。

　　1983 年拜在少林寺住持素喜法師和著名武僧素法大師門下學藝，成為大師的關門弟子，後經素法大師引薦，又隨螳螂拳一代宗師李占元、金剛力功于憲華等大師學藝。在中國鄭州國際少林武術節、全國武林精英大賽、全國武術演武大會等比賽中 6 次獲得少林武術冠軍；在中華傳統武術精粹大賽中獲得了象徵少林武術最高榮譽的「達摩杯」一座。他主講示範的 36 集《少林傳統功夫》教學片已由人民體育音像出版社出版發行。他曾多次率團出訪海外，在國際武術界享有較高聲譽。

　　他創辦的孟州少林武術院，現已發展成爲豫北地區最大的以學習文化爲主、以武術爲辦學特色的封閉式、寄宿制學校，是中國十大武術教育基地之一。

Brief Introduction to the Author

Geng Jun（also named Shidejun in Buddhism）, born in Mengzhou City of Henan Province, November 1968, is a Bud–dhist disciple of the 31st generation, the 7th section of Chinese Wu shu, national "Shijia" Wu shu coach, Vice Secretary General of China Shaolin Wu shu Research Society, standing committee member of 10th Political Consultative Conference of Jiaozuo City, invited General Kungfu Coach of special police of Jinan Military District, visiting professor of Luoyang Normal University, and Board Chairman of Yingcai Education Group. In 1989, he estab–lished Mengzhou Shaolin Wu shu Institute; in 2001, he estab –lished Yingcai Bilingual School・He has been successively awarded honorable titles of "Excellent Youth News Celebrity of Henan Province" "State Excellent Wu shu Educationalist" etc.

In 1983, he learned Wu shu from Suxi Rabbi, the Abbot of Shaolin Temple, and Grandmaster Sufa, a famous Wu shu monk, and became the last disciple of the

Grandmaster. Then recom – mended by Grandmaster Sufa, he learned Wu shu from masters such as Li Zhanyuan, great master of mantis boxing, and Yu Xianhua who specializes in Jingangli gong. He won the Shaolin Wu shu champion for 6 times in China Zhengzhou International Wu shu Festival, National Competition of Wu lin Elites, National Wu shu Performance Conference, etc. and one "Damo Trophy" that symbolizes the highest honor of Shaolin Wu shu in Chinese Traditional Wu shu Succinct Competition. 36 volumes teaching VCD of Shaolin Traditional Wu shu has been published and is – sued by People's Sports Audio Visual Publishing House. He has led delegations to visit overseas for many times, enjoying high reputation in the martial art circle of the world.

Mengzhou Shaolin Wu shu Institute, established by him, has developed into the largest enclosed type boarding school of Yubei (north of Henan Province) area, which takes knowledge as primary and Wu shu as distinctiveness, also one of China's top ten Wu shu education bases.

序　言

中華武術源遠流長，門類繁多。

少林武術源自嵩山少林寺，因寺齊名，是我國拳系中著名的流派之一。少林寺自北魏太和十九年建寺以來，已有一千五百多年的歷史。而少林武術也決不是哪一人哪一僧所獨創，它是歷代僧俗歷經漫長的生活歷程，根據生活所需逐步豐富完善而成。

據少林寺志記載許多少林僧人在出家之前就精通武術或慕少林之名而來或迫於生計或看破紅塵等諸多原因削髮爲僧投奔少林，少林寺歷來倡武，並經常派武僧下山，雲遊四方尋師學藝。還請武林高手到寺，如宋朝的福居禪師曾邀集十八家武林名家到寺切磋技藝，推動了少林武術的發展，使少林武術得諸家之長。

本書作者自幼習武，師承素喜、素法和螳螂拳李占元等多位名家，當年如饑似渴在少林寺研習功夫，曾多次在國內外大賽中獲獎。創辦的孟州少林武術院亦是全國著名的武術院校之一，他示範主講的 36 集《少林傳統功夫》教學 VCD 已由人民體育音像出版社發行。

本套叢書的三十多個少林傳統套路和實戰技法是少

七星螳螂拳 梅花路

林武術的主要內容，部分還是作者獨到心得，很值得一讀，該書還採用漢英文對照，使外國愛好者無語言障礙，爲少林武術走向世界做出了自己的貢獻，亦是可喜可賀之事。

張耀庭題
甲申秋月

Preface

序言

Chinese Wushu is originated from ancient time and has a long history, it has various styles.

Shaolin Wushu named from the Shaolin Temple of Songshan Mountain, it is one of the famous styles in the Chinese boxing genre. Shaolin temple has more than 1500 years of history since its establishment in the 19th year of North Wei Taihe Dynasty. No one genre of Shaolin Wushu is created solely by any person or monk, but completed gradually by Buddhist monks and common people from generation to generation through long–lasting living course according to the requirements of life. As recording of Record of Shaolin Temple, many Shaolin Buddhist monks had already got a mastery of Wushu before they became a Buddhist monk, they came to Shaolin for tonsure to be a Buddhist monk due to many reasons such as admiring for the name of Shaolin, or by force of life or seeing through thevanity of life. The Shaolin Temple always promotes Wushu and frequently appoints Wushu Buddhist monks to go down the mountain to roam around for searching masters and learning Wushu from them. It also invites

Wushu experts to come to the temple, such as Buddhist monk Fuju of Song Dynasty, it once invited Wushu famous exports of 18 schools to come to the temple to make skill interchange, which promoted the development of Shaolin Wushu and made it absorb advantages of all other schools.

The author learned from many famous exports such as Suxi, Sufa and Li Zhanyuan of Mantis Boxing, he studied Chinese boxing eagerly in Shaolin Temple, and got lots of awards both at home and abroad, he also set up the Mengzhou Shaolin Wushu Institute, which is one of the most famous Wushu institutes around China. He makes demonstration and teaching in the 36 volumes teaching VCD of Shaolin Traditional Wushu, which have been published by Peoples sports Audio Visual publishing house.

There are more than 30 traditional Shaolin routines and practical techniques in this series of books, which are the main content of Shaolin Wushu, and part of which is the original things learned by the author, it is worthy of reading. The series books adopt Chinese and English versions, make foreign fans have no language barrier, and make contribution to Shaolin Wushu going to the world, which is delighting and congratulating thing.

Titled by Zhang Yaoting

目　錄
Contents

七星螳螂拳 梅花路

說　明

（一）為了表述清楚，以圖像和文字對動作作了分解說明，練習時應力求連貫銜接。

（二）在文字說明中，除特別說明外，不論先寫或後寫身體的某一部分，各運動部位都要求協調活動、連貫銜接，切勿先後割裂。

（三）動作方向轉變以人體為準，標明前後左右。

（四）圖上的線條是表明這一動作到下一動作經過的線路及部位。左手、左腳及左轉均為虛線（┈┈►）；右手、右腳及右轉均為實線（──►）。

Instructions

(i) In order to explain clearly figures and words are used to describe the actions in multi steps. Try to keep coherent when exercising.

(ii) In the word instruction, unless special instruction, each action part of the body shall act harmoniously and join coherently no matter it is written first or last, please do not separate the actions.

(iii) The action direction shall be turned taking body as standard, which is marked with front, back, left or right.

(iv) The line in the figure shows the route and position from this action to the next action. The left hand, left foot and turn left are all showed in broken line (------►) ; the right hand, right foot and turn right are all showed in real line (——►) .

基本步型與基本手型
Basic stances and Basic hand forms

圖 1

圖 2

圖 3

圖 4

圖 5

圖 6

圖 7

圖 8

圖 9

圖 10

圖 11

圖 12

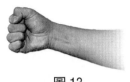

圖 13

圖 14

圖 15

圖 16

圖 17

圖 18

圖 19

圖 20

圖 21

基本步型與基本手型

基本步型

少林武術中常見的步型有：弓步、馬步、仆步、虛步、歇步、坐盤步、丁步、併步、七星步、跪步、高虛步、翹腳步 12 種。

弓步：俗稱弓箭步。兩腿前後站立，兩腳相距本人腳長的 4～5 倍；前腿屈至大腿接近水平，腳尖微內扣不超過 5°；後腿伸膝挺直，腳掌內扣 45°。（圖 1）

馬步：俗稱騎馬步。兩腳開立，相距本人腳長的 3～3.5 倍，兩腳尖朝前；屈膝下蹲大腿接近水平，膝蓋與兩腳尖上下成一條線。（圖 2）

仆步：俗稱單叉，一腿屈膝全蹲，大腿貼緊小腿，膝微外展，另一腿直伸平仆接近地面，腳掌扣緊與小腿成 90°夾角。（圖 3）

虛步：又稱寒雞步。兩腳前後站立，前後相距本人腳長的 2 倍；重心移至後腿，後腿屈膝下蹲至大腿接近水平，腳掌外擺 45°；前腿腳尖點地，兩膝相距 10 公分。（圖 4）

歇步：兩腿左右交叉，靠近全蹲；前腳全腳掌著地，腳尖外展，後腳腳前掌著地，臀部微坐於後腿小腿上。（圖 5）

坐盤步：在歇步的形狀下，坐於地上，後腿的大小腿外側和腳背均著地。（圖 6）

丁步：兩腿併立，屈膝下蹲，大腿接近水平，一腳尖點地靠近另一腳內側腳窩處。（圖7）

併步：兩腿併立，屈膝下蹲，大腿接近水平。（圖8）

七星步：七星步是少林七星拳和大洪拳中獨有的步型。一腳內側腳窩內扣於另一腳腳尖，兩腿屈膝下蹲，接近水平。（圖9）

跪步：又稱小蹬山步。兩腳前後站立，相距本人腳長的2.5倍，前腿屈膝下蹲，後腿下跪，接近地面，後腳腳跟離地。（圖10）

高虛步：又稱高點步。兩腳前後站立，重心後移，後腿腳尖外擺45°，前腿腳尖點地，兩腳尖相距一腳距離。（圖11）

翹腳步：在七星螳螂拳中又稱七星步，兩腿前後站立，相距本人腳長的1.5倍，後腳尖外擺45°，屈膝下蹲，前腿直伸，腳跟著地，腳尖微內扣。（圖12）

基本手型

少林武術中常見的手型有拳、掌、鉤3種。

拳：

分為平拳和透心拳。

平拳：平拳是武術中較普遍的一種拳型，又稱方拳。四指屈向手心握緊，拇指橫屈扣緊食指。（圖

13）

　　透心拳：此拳主要用於打擊心窩處，故名。四指併攏捲握，中指突出拳面，拇指扣緊抵壓中指梢節處。（圖14）

　　掌：

　　分為柳葉掌、八字掌、虎爪掌、鷹爪掌、鉗指掌。

　　柳葉掌：四指併立，拇指內扣。（圖15）

　　八字掌：四指併立，拇指張開。（圖16）

　　虎爪掌：五指分開，彎曲如鉤，形同虎爪。（圖17）

　　鷹爪掌：又稱鎖喉手，拇指內扣，小指和無名指彎曲扣於掌心處，食指和中指分開內扣。（圖18）

　　鉗指掌：五指分開，掌心內含。（圖19）

　　鉤：

　　分為鉤手和螳螂鉤。

　　鉤手：屈腕，五指自然內合，指尖相攏。此鉤使用較廣，武術中提到的鉤均為此鉤。（圖20）

　　螳螂鉤：又稱螳螂爪，屈腕成腕部上凸，無名指、小指屈指內握，食指、中指內扣，拇指梢端按貼於食指中節。（圖21）

Basic stances

Usual stances in Shaolin Wushu are: bow stance, horse stance, crouch stance, empty stance, rest stance, cross – legged sitting, T – stance, feet – together stance, seven – star stance, kneel stance, high empty stance, and toes – raising stance, these twelve kinds.

Bow stance: commonly named bow – and – arrow stance. Two feet stand in tandem, the distance between two feet is about four or five times of length of one's foot; the front leg bends to the extent of the thigh nearly horizontal with toes slightly turned inward by less than 5°; the back leg stretches straight with the sole turned inward by 45°. (Figure 1)

Horse stance: commonly named riding step. two feet stand apart, the distance between two feet is 3~3.5 times of length of one's foot, with tiptoes turned forward; bend knees to squat downward, with thighs nearly horizontal, knees and two tiptoes in line. (Figure 2)

Crouch stance: commonly named single split. Bend the knee of one leg and squat entirely with thigh very close to lower leg and knee outspread slightly; straighten the other leg and crouch horizontally close to floor, keep the sole turned inward and forming an included angle of 90° with lower leg. (Figure 3)

Empty stance: also named cold – chicken stance. Two feet stand in tandem, the distance between two feet is 2 times of

七星螳螂拳
梅花路

length of one's foot; transfer the barycenter to back leg, bend the knee of the back leg and squat downward to the extent of the thigh nearly horizontal, with the sole turned outward by 45°; keep the tiptoe of front leg on the ground, with distance between two knees of 10cm. (Figure 4)

Rest stance: cross the two legs at left and right, keep them close and entirely squat; keep the whole sole of the front foot on the ground with tiptoes turned outward, the front sole of the back foot on the ground, and buttocks slightly seated on the lower leg of the back leg. (Figure 5)

Cross-legged sitting: in the posture of rest stance, sit on the ground, with the outer sides of the thigh and lower leg of the back leg and instep on the ground. (Figure 6)

T-stance: two legs stand with feet together, bend knees and squat to the extent of the thighs nearly horizontal, with one tiptoe on the ground and close to inner side of the fossa of the other foot. (Figure 7)

Feet-together stance: two legs stand with feet together, bend knees and squat to the extent of the thigh nearly horizontal. (Figure 8)

Seven-star stance: Seven-star step is a unique step form in Shaolin Seven-star Boxing and Major Flood Boxing. Keep the inner side of the fossa of one foot turned inward onto tiptoe of the other foot, bend two knees and squat nearly horizontal. (Figure 9)

Kneel stance: also named small mountaineering stance. Two feet stand in tandem, the distance between two feet is 2.5

times of length of one´s foot, bend knee of the front leg and squat, kneel the back leg close to the floor, with the heel of back foot off the floor. (Figure 10)

High empty stance: also named high point stance. Two feet stand in tandem. Transfer the barycenter backward, turn the tiptoe of the back leg outward by 45°, with tiptoe of front leg on the ground, and the distance between two tiptoes is length of one foot. (Figure 11)

Toes –raising stance: also named seven –star stance in Seven –star Mantis Boxing. Two legs stand in tandem, and the distance between two legs is 1.5 times of length of one´s foot. Keep the tiptoe of back leg turned outward by 45°, bend knees and squat, straighten the front leg with heel on the ground and tiptoe turned inward slightly. (Figure 12)

Basic hand forms

Usual hand forms in Shaolin Wushu are: fist, palm and hook, these three kinds.

Fist: classified into straight fist and heart–penetrating fist.

Flat fist: a rather common fist form in Wushu, also named square fist. Hold the four fingers tightly toward the palm, and horizontally bend the thumb to button up the fore finger. (Figure 13)

Heart –penetrating fist: mainly used for striking the heart part. Put four fingers together and coil –hold them, the middle finger thrusts out the striking surface of the fist, the thumb

buttons up and presses the end and joint of the middle finger. (Figure 14)

Palm: classified into willow leaf palm, splay palm, tiger's claw palm, eagle's claw palm, fingers clamping palm.

Willow leaf palm: palm with four fingers up and thumb turned inward. (Figure 15)

Eight–shape palm: palm with four fingers up and thumb splay. (Figure 16)

Tiger's claw palm: palm with five fingers apart, bent as hook and like tiger's claw. (Figure 17)

Eagle's claw palm: also named throat locking hand, with the thumb turned inward, the little finger and middle finger turned onto palm, fore finger and middle finger apart and turned inward. (Figure 18)

Fingers clamp palm: palm with five fingers apart and palm drawn in. (Figure 19)

Hook: classified into hook hand and mantis hook.

Hook hand: bend the wrist, five fingers drawn in naturally with fingertips together. This hook is used in wide range, the hook mentioned in Wushu refers to this. (Figure 20)

Mantis hook: also named mantis' claw, bend wrist into wrist bulge upward, the ring finger and little finger bend to hold inward, with fore finger and fore middle finger turned inward and end of thumb pressed on the middle joint of the fore finger. (Figure 21)

梅花路套路簡介
Brief Introduction to the Routine Plum Blossom

　　七星螳螂拳是清初拳師王郎在研究螳螂捕蟬時運用兩臂劈、砍、刁、閃的捕鬥技巧而創編的一種象形拳法。後王郎入少林寺３年，向寺僧傳授螳螂拳法。梅花路是七星螳螂拳其中的一個套路，該套路剛柔並濟、長短互用、手到腳到、貫穿緊湊、節奏明快、勁整力圓、周身相合、勾摟纏封、變化無窮。

　　Seven－star mantis boxing is a kind of imitation boxing, which was developed and compiled by Wang Lang, a boxer at early Qing Dynasty, applying the capturing and fighting skills of the two arms when he researched the scene of mantis capturing cicada. Later, Wang Lang stayed at Shaolin Temple for 3 years, and taught mantis boxing to the monks of temple. Plum Blossom Routine is one of the routines in seven－star mantis boxing, which uses the temper force with grace, both long and short actions, harmonious and consistent actions of the hands and feet, forthright rhythm, integral strength and complete force, the actions of hook, grasp, twining and closing, being coherent, compact and most changeful.

梅花路套路動作名稱
Action Names of Routine Plum Blossom

第一段　Section One

1. 預備勢　Preparatory position
2. 螳螂雙封手　Mantis closes up two hands
3. 左封右秘肘　Left wrap and right secret elbow
4. 纏龍護眼打　Intertwining dragon guards eyes and strikes
5. 左擒右蹬踏　Left capture and right stamp
6. 霸王摘盔　Overlord puts off the armature
7. 擒髮挫嘴巴　Seize hair and jab mouth
8. 雙叫雙幫肘　Helping double elbows with double calls
9. 二龍戲珠　Two dragons plays pearl
10. 偷展磨盤打　Stretch secretly and millstones strike
11. 虎抱頭窩心腳　Tiger holds head and kick toward heart
12. 馬步劈砸　Hack and pound in horse stance
13. 左封右崩　Left wrap and right snap
14. 鳳凰三點頭　Phoenix nods three times
15. 臨行鴛鴦腳　Mandarin-duck foot before leaving
16. 轉身回馬鞭　Turn body and whip backward

梅花路套路動作名稱

第二段　Section Two

17. 右採迎面圈　Pick rightward for head-on circle
18. 幫肘　Helping elbow
19. 七星拳　Seven-star fist
20. 左封右崩　Left wrap and right snap
21. 拉弓捶　Bow-pulling hammer
22. 左採迎面圈　Pick leftward for head-on circle
23. 幫肘　Helping elbow
24. 二龍戲珠　Two dragons play pearl
25. 偷展磨盤打　Stretch secretly and the millstones strike
26. 纏龍鎖口窩心腳　Intertwining dragon locks mouth and kick toward heart
27. 馬步劈砸　Hack and pound in horse stance
28. 左封右崩　Left wrap and right snap
29. 轉身護眼指　Turn body and jab eyes
30. 螳螂雙封手　Mantis closes up hands

第三段　Section Three

31. 左右護腿　Guard left and right legs
32. 起身貫耳　Rise body to strike ears
33. 落地下掃襠　Land on ground to sweep crotch
34. 進步打中堂　Step forward to strike Zhongtang
35. 採手右崩點　Pick hand and snap point

36. 偷展磨盤打　Stretch secretly and millstones strike

37. 轉身左封右崩　Left wrap and right snap with body turn

38. 叫手擒摔　Call hands for capturing throw

39. 左封右圈捶　Left wrap and right circular hammer

40. 鳳凰三點頭　Phoenix nods three times

41. 臨行鴛鴦腳　Mandarin–duck foot before leaving

42. 雙幫肘　Double helping elbows

第四段　Section Four

43. 退步翻車　Step back and turn over

44. 進步轆轤靠　Step forward and lean with windlass

45. 左封右陽拳　left wrap and right Yang fist

46. 雙分左格肘　Double parting and parrying with left elbow

47. 雙分右格肘　Double parting and parrying with right elbow

48. 左擒右蹬踏　Left capture and right stamp

49. 反掌擊面　Turn over palm to hit face

50. 雙分左閉手　Double parting and left hand close–up

51. 雙分右閉手　Double parting and right hand close–up

52. 雙封閉門腳　Double wraps and close–up foot

53. 螳螂雙封手　Mantis close–up hands

54. 收勢　Closing form

梅花路套路動作圖解
Action Illustrtion of Routine Plum Blossom

圖1

第一段　Section One

1. 預備勢　Preparatory position

(1)兩腳併立；兩手自然下垂，五指併攏，貼於體側；目視前方。（圖1）

(1) Stand with feet together. Two hands hang naturally, five fingers put together and keep close to the two sides of the body. Eyes look forward.〔Figure 1〕

七星螳螂拳　梅花路

圖 2

(2)兩手上提變拳，抱於兩腰間，拳心向上；目視左方。（圖 2）。

要點：身體正立，挺胸塌腰，頭正頸直。挺胸收腹，抱拳迅速。

(2) Two hands lift upward and change into fists, then hold on the waist with the fist-palm up. Eyes look leftward. ﹝ Figure 2 ﹞

Key points: Stand erect, head upright, chest out and abdomen in. Lift the chest, draw in the abdomen and hold fists quickly.

圖 3

2. 螳螂雙封手　Mantis closes up two hands

(1)接上勢。身體左轉 90°，右腳提起向後撤一步；同時，右拳變掌，掌心向下，從後向身前畫掌；左拳變掌向下插掌，掌心向下，與右前臂相交於腹前；目視兩掌。（圖 3）

(1) Follow the above posture, turn the body 90° to the left, the right foot lifts upward and takes a step backward. At the same time, change the right fist into palm, pull the palm back then swing forward with the palm down, change the left one into palm and insert it downward with the palm down, crossing with the right forearm in front of the abdomen. Eyes look at two palms. (Figure 3)

圖4

（2）上動不停。身體略向後傾斜；同時，兩臂屈肘，兩掌在胸前翻轉絞手，右掌心向上，掌指向右，高與頷平；左掌心向右，掌指向後，略高於右手；目視前方。（圖4）

(2) Keep the above action, keep the body backward aslant. At the same time, bend the elbows of two arms, turn over the two palms and twine up the hands in front of the chest. Keep the right palm up, the fingers rightward, at the jaw height, while the left palm rightward, the fingers backward, higher than the right hand slightly. Eyes look forward.（Figure 4）

圖 5

(3)上動不停。重心略前移；同時，右掌前探，虎
口向上，掌心向前，高與肩平；左掌護於右肩前，掌
心向右，掌指向後；目視右掌。（圖5）

(3) Keep the above action, move the barycenter forwardly
slightly. At the same time, the right palm stretch forward with
the palm forward at the shoulder level, the left palm guards in
front of the right shoulder with the palm rightward and the
fingers backward. Eyes look at the right palm.〔Figure 5〕

圖 6

　　(4)上動不停。右臂屈肘，右掌變為螳螂鉤，吊腕回拉於胸前，鉤尖向下；同時，左掌前伸成掌指向前，掌心向下，高與肩平；目視左掌。（圖6）

　　(4) Keep the above action, bend the elbow of the right arm, change the right palm into mantis hook and hang the wrist to draw back in front of the chest with the hook-tip down. At the same time, stretch the left palm ahead with the fingers forward, the palm down at the shoulder level. Eyes look at the left palm. (Figure 6)

圖 7

(5)上動不停。左腳向後退半步，重心後移成左虛步；同時，左臂屈肘，左掌變為螳螂鈎，吊腕回拉於左膝上方，鈎尖向下，高與肩平；目視前方。（圖7）

(5) Keep the above action, the left foot takes a half step backward, shift, the barycenter backward into the left empty stance. At the same time, bend the elbow of the left arm, change the left palm into mantis hook and hang the wrist to draw back upon the left knee with the hook-tip down at the shoulder level. Eyes look forward.（Figure 7）

圖 8

3. 左封右秘肘
Left wrap and right secret elbow

(1)接上勢。身體提起，左腳踏實，身體略微右轉；同時，左鉤手由外向裏、向上畫，鉤尖向右，略高於肩；右鉤手收回腰間，鉤尖向前；目視前方。（圖 8）

梅
花
路
套
路
動
作
圖
解

(1) Follow the above posture, the body lifts up, the left foot stamps firmly, the body turns to the left slightly. At the same time, pull the left hook hand inward and upward with the hook – tip rightward, higher than the shoulders slightly, draw back the right one on the waist with the hook –tip forward. Eyes look forward. (Figure 8)

圖9

　　(2)上動不停。左腳向前上半步，隨即重心前移，向下蹲身成蹬山步；同時，左手螳螂鉤經胸前向下、向左勾摟，鉤尖向外，高與頭頂平；右鉤手由後向前反撩至左膝前，鉤尖向右下方，高與膝平；上身略向左傾斜；目視前方。（圖9、圖9附圖）

圖 9 附圖

(2) Keep the above action, the left foot takes a half step forward, then shift the barycenter forward, squat the body down into mountaineering step. At the same time, draw and grab the mantis hook of the left hand downward and leftward with the hook–tip outward at the head top level. The right hook hand lifts in reverse from in front of the left knee with the hook–tip down rightward at the knee level. Keep the upper part of the body leftward aslant slightly. Eyes look forward. 〔Figure 9, Attached figure 9〕

七
星
螳
螂
拳
梅
花
路

圖 10

4. 纏龍護眼打
Intertwining dragon guards eyes and strikes

(1)接上勢。身體提起；右鉤手變掌，向外翻腕刁抓變為螳螂鉤，鉤尖向下，高與眉齊；同時，左鉤手由外向裏收於腰間，鉤尖向右。目視右鉤手。（圖10）

(1) Follow the above posture, raise the body, change the right hook hand into palm and turn the wrist outward to grab into mantis hook with the hook–tip down at the eyebrow level, At the same time, draw the left one inward from outside and hold on the waist with the hook–tip rightward. Eyes look at the right hook hand.（Figure 10）

圖 11

(2)上動不停。重心向前移至左腿，右腿提膝過
胯，左腿獨立；同時，右鉤手向後鉤拉，鉤尖向下，
略高於肩；左鉤手變掌向前平推，掌心向前，掌指向
上，高與肩平；目視左掌。（圖 11）

(2) Keep the above action, shift the barycenter forward onto
the left leg, lift the right knee higher than the hip with the left leg
standing alone. At the same time, draw the right hook hand
backward with the hook‐tip down and higher than the shoulder
slightly, change the left one into palm and push forward
horizontally with the palm forward and the fingers up at the
shoulder level. Eyes look at the left palm.〔Figure 11〕

圖 12

5. 左擒右蹬踏　Left capture and right stamp

(1)接上勢。右鉤手向外翻腕變掌，向左前方畫出，掌指向下，掌心向前，略低於肩；同時，左臂屈肘，左掌掌心向下，向右穿掌，置於右肘下，虎口向裏，掌心向下；目視右掌。（圖 12）

(1)Follow the above posture, turn over the wrist of the right hook hand into palm and pull it left forward with the fingers down and the palm forward, lower than the shoulder slightly. At the same time, bend the left elbow and thread out the left palm downward and rightward with the palm down, place it under the right elbow, keep the tiger′s mouth inward and the palm down. Eyes look at the right palm.（Figure 12）

梅花路套路動作圖解

圖 13

(2)上動不停。右腿向前伸直；同時，右掌向後擺掌，虎口向外，掌指向後，略高於胯；左掌從右肘下向前推出，掌心向外，掌指向前，高與肩平；目視右腳。（圖 13）

(2) Keep the above action, stretch the right leg straight forward. At the same time, swing the right palm backward, keep the tiger´s mouth outward and the fingers backward, higher than the hip slightly, push the left palm forward from the right elbow, keep the palm outward and the fingers forward at the shoulder height. Eyes look at the right foot. 〔Figure 13〕

七星螳螂拳 梅花路

圖 14

　　(3)上動不停。身略左轉，右腿向右後側蹬踏地面落地，成左弓步；同時，左掌變拳收抱於腰間；右掌隨身左轉，自右向左橫掌撩擊擺於身體右側，掌心向前，掌指向斜下方，高與左膝平；目視右掌。（圖 14）

梅花路套路動作圖解

(3) Keep the above action, the body turns to the left slightly, the right leg kicks right backward and stamps to the ground into the left bow stance. At the same time, change the left palm into fist and hold on the waist, turn the right one with the body and horizontally swing it from right to the left on the right side of the body, keep the palm forward and the fingers down aslant at the left knee level. Eyes look at the right palm. 〔Figure 14〕

圖 15

6. 霸王摘盔
Overlord puts off the armature

　　(1)接上勢。身體右轉 90°，重心移至右腿；同時，右掌上翻為掌心向上，右臂隨即向下、向後擺至後方，掌心向外，掌指向後，高與肩平；左拳變掌，從外向前擺掌，掌心向上，掌指向前，高與肩平；目視前方。（圖 15）

(1)Follow the above posture, turn the body 90° to the right, move the barycenter to the right leg. At the same time, turn the right palm with the palm up, then swing the right arm downward and backward to the back side, keep the palm outward and the fingers backward at the shoulder height, change the left fist into palm and swing it forward from outside, keep the palm up and the fingers forward at the shoulder height. Eyes look forward. (Figure 15)

七星螳螂拳　梅花路

圖 16

(2)上動不停。右腿獨立，左腿提起，腳尖內扣於右膝前；同時，左臂屈肘，左掌上托，掌指向前，掌心向上；右臂屈肘，右掌由後向前翻掌，掌心向下，掌指向前，高與肩平，兩掌前後相照；目視前方。（圖 16）

(2)Keep the above action, the right leg stands alone, the left one lifts up, toes turn inward in front of the right knee. At the same time, bend the left elbow, hold the left palm upward with the fingers forward and the palm up, bend the right elbow and turn over the right palm forward from back, keep the palm down and the fingers forward at the shoulder height. Keep the two palms opposite. Eyes look forward. (Figure 16)

圖 17

7. 擒髮挫嘴巴　Seize hair and jab mouth

接上勢。左腳向前上一步，右腳隨即向前跟半步，身體下蹲成蹬山步；同時，右掌向前挫擊，掌心向下，掌指向前，高與耳平；左掌回收迎擊右掌後於右肘內側，掌心向上，掌指向前；目視前方。（圖17）

Follow the above posture, the left foot takes a step forward, then the right one follows a half step forward, the body squats into mountaineering step. At the same time, the right palm jabs forward, keep the palm downward and the fingers forward at the ear level, draw back the left one to counterpunch the right palm and place it at the inner side of the right elbow, with the palm up and the fingers forward. Eyes look forward.〔Figure 17〕

圖 18

8. 雙叫雙幫肘
Helping double elbows with double calls

（1）接上勢。右臂微屈，右掌翻腕外旋變拳，拳心向上，拳面向前，略低於肩；同時，左掌變拳內旋，拳心貼於右前臂上，拳面向右；目視左拳。（圖 18）

（1）Follow the above posture, slightly bend the right arm, turn the right palm and rotate it outward to change into fist, with the palm side up and the fist–plane forward, slightly lower than the shoulder. At the same time, change the left palm into fist and rotate it inward, keep the fist–palm close to the right forearm with the fist–face rightward. Eyes look at the left fist.（Figure 18）

圖 19

(2)上動不停。重心前移至左腿，右腿提起，左腿獨立，身略後仰；同時，屈右臂，右拳內旋成拳眼向裏，拳心向下；左拳附於右臂內側；目視前方。（圖19）

(2) Keep the above action, shift the barycenter forward onto the left leg, the right leg lifts up, the left one stands alone, keep the body backward with face upward. At the same time, bend the right arm, rotate the right fist inward with the fist−holes inward and the fist−palm, down, keep the left fist close to the inner side of the right arm. Eyes look forward.〔Figure 19〕

圖 20

　　⑶上動不停。右腳向前上一步，隨即左腳向前跟步，身體下蹲成蹬山步；同時，左拳附於右臂內側與右臂向前橫推，兩拳心向下，拳眼向裏；目視前方。（圖 20）

　　⑶Keep the above action, the right foot takes a step forward, then the left one follows half a step forward, the body squats into mountaineering step. At the same time, keep the left fist close to the inner side of the right arm, horizontally push it together with the right arm forward, the left fist behind the right one, with the two fist −palms down and the fist −holes inward. Eyes look forward.（Figure 20）

圖 21

9. 二龍戲珠   Two dragons plays pearl

(1)接上勢。左拳回抱於腰間，拳心向上；同時，右拳變掌，向前、向外摟，掌心向前，掌指向左，高與肩平；目視右掌。（圖 21）

(1) Follow the above posture, draw back the left fist and hold on the waist with the fist–palm up. At the same time, change the right fist into palm and grab forward and outward, with the palm forward and the fingers leftward at the shoulder level. Eyes look at the right palm.（Figure 21）

圖 22

（2）上動不停。左腳向前挪半步，身體右轉 90°成歇步；同時，右掌外摟變拳，收抱於腰間；左拳食指、中指分開前伸，成剪子手向前平插，高與肩平；目視左手兩指。（圖 22）

(2) Keep the above action, the left foot takes a half-step forward, turn the body 90° to the right into the rest stance. At the same time, the right palm grabs outward and change into fist, draw back and hold on the waist, the tiger's mouth and stretch forward into scissors hand and inserts forward horizontally, at the shoulder height. Eyes look at such two fingers of the left hand.（Figure 22）

圖 23

10. 偷展磨盤打
Stretch secretly and millstones Strike

(1)接上勢。兩腿起身直立，重心移至右腳成叉步；同時，左臂外旋，左手變掌向前上方穿掌，掌指向前，高與眼平；目視左掌。（圖 23）

(1) Follow the above posture, stand up with the two legs erective, move the barycenter to the right foot into the cross stance. At the same time, the left arm rotates outward, change the left hand into palm and thread upward ahead with the fingers forward at the eye height. Eyes look at the left palm.（Figure 23）

七星螳螂拳　梅花路

圖24

　　(2)上動不停。左腳向前上一步，隨即右腳跟半步，身體下蹲成蹬山步；同時，左掌變拳，內旋下翻，拳心向下，拳面向前，高與眼平；右拳變掌，向左下方推掌至左膝外側，掌心向左，虎口向上，掌指向前；目視前方。（圖24）

(2) Keep the above action, the left foot takes a step forward, then the right one follows a half −step, the body squats into mountaineering step. At the same time, change the left palm into fist and rotate it inward and turn downward, keep the fist−palm down and the fist−plane forward at the eye level, and change the right fist into palm and horizontally push it left downward to the outer side of the left knee, with the palm leftward, part of the hand between the tiger's mouth upward and the fingers forward. Eyes look forward. (Figure 24)

圖 25

11. 虎抱頭窩心腳
Tiger holds head and kick toward heart

(1)接上勢。身體提起，重心前移至左腿；同時，左拳收抱於腰間；目視前方。（圖 25）

(1) Follow the above step, raise the body and shift the barycenter forward to the left leg. At the same time, draw back the left fist and hold on the waist. Eyes look forward.〔Figure 25〕

梅花路套路動作圖解

圖 26

　(2)上動不停。右腿提起向前蹬腳；同時，右掌變
拳，經胸前上架於頭頂，拳心向上，拳眼向前；左拳
變掌，向前平推，掌心向前，掌指向上，高與肩平；
目視左掌。（圖 26）

　(2) Keep the above action, the right leg lifts up and kicks
forward with heel. At the same time, change the right palm into
fist and parry it on the head top with the fist－palm up and the
fist－hole forward, change the left fist into palm and horizontally
push forward with the palm forward and the fingers up at the
shoulder height. Eyes look at the left palm.（Figure 26）

圖 27

12. 馬步劈砸
Hack and pound in horse stance

接上勢。身體左轉 90°，落右腳成馬步；同時，右臂屈肘，右拳經胸前從上向下劈拳，拳心向裏，拳眼向上，略高於右膝；左掌向上迎擊右前臂內側，掌心貼於右肘內側，掌指向上；目視右拳。（圖 27、圖 27附圖）

要點：馬步和劈拳同步完成，劈拳迅猛有力，力達拳輪。

梅花路套路動作圖解

圖 27 附圖

Follow the above posture, turn the body 90° to the left, the right foot falls into horse stance. At the same time, bend the right elbow, hack with the right fist from up to down through the front of the chest, keep the fist –palm inward and the fist –hole up, slightly higher than the right knee, lift the left fist upward to counterpunch the inner side of the right forearm, keep the palm side close to the inner side of the right elbow with the fingers upward. Eyes look at the right fist. (Figure 27, Attached Figure 27)

Key points: Complete the horse stance and hacking of the fist simultaneously, hacking with the fist shall be rapid and forceful with the strength reaching the fist wheel.

圖 28

13. 左封右崩　Left wrap and right snap

(1)接上勢。身體右轉 90°成右弓步；同時，右拳收抱於腰間；左掌由外向裏封抓變拳，拳心向下，拳面向右，高與肩平；目視前方。（圖 28）

(1) Keep the above posture, turn body 90° to the right, forming a right bow stance. At the same, draw right fist back and hold it on the waist, wrap left palm from exterior to interior and change it into fist with fist –palm down word and fist –plane rightward, at should height. Eyes look forward. (Figure 28)

圖 29

(2)上動不停。右拳經左前臂內側向前崩拳，拳面向上，拳眼向右，高與鼻齊；同時，左拳屈臂置於右肘下，拳心向下，拳面向右；目視前方。（圖 29）

(2) Keep the above action, the right fist snaps forward through the inner side of the left forearm, keep the fist‑plane up and the fist‑hole rightward at the nose level. At the same time, bend the left arm and place the left fist under the right elbow with the fist‑palm down and the fist‑plane rightward. Eyes look forward.（Figure 29）

圖 30

14. 鳳凰三點頭　Phoenix nods three times

(1)接上勢。右拳變掌外摟後仍變拳收抱於腰間；同時，左拳向前平沖，拳心向下，拳眼向右，高與肩平；目視左拳。（圖 30）

(1) Follow the above posture, change the right fist into palm and grab outward into fist, draw back and hold on the waist. At the same time, the left fist punches forward horizontally, with the fist–palm down and the fist–hole rightward at the shoulder height. Eyes look at the left fist. (Figure 30)

圖 31

(2)上動不停。左拳收抱於腰間，拳心向上；同時，右拳向前平沖，拳面向前，拳心向下，高與肩平；目視右拳。（圖 31）

(2) Keep the above action, draw back and hold the left fist on the waist with the fist－palm up. At the same time, the right fist punches forward horizontally, with the fist－plane forward and the fist－palm down at the shoulder height. Eyes look at the right fist.（Figure 31）

七星螳螂拳 梅花路

圖 32

(3)上動不停。右拳收抱於腰間，拳心向上；同時，左拳向前平沖，拳心向下，高與肩平；目視左拳。（圖 32）

(3) Keep the above action, draw back and hold the right fist on the waist with the fist–palm up. At the same time, the left fist strikes forward horizontally with the fist –palm down at the shoulder height. Eyes look at the left fist. (Figure 32)

梅花路套路動作圖解

圖 33

15. 臨行鴛鴦腳
Mandarin-duck foot before leaving

(1)接上勢。起身，左轉 90°；同時，右臂屈肘向上抬起，右拳拳心向下，拳眼貼於左胸前，略低於肩；左臂向下、向後擺拳置於左胯側，拳心向後，拳眼向下；目視右前方。（圖 33、圖 33 附圖）

圖 33 附圖

(1) Follow the above posture, raise the body and turn it 90° to the left. At the same time, bend the right arm and lift up the right elbow, with the fist–palm down and the fist–hole close to the front of the left chest, slightly lower than the shoulder. The left arm swings the fist downward and backward and places it at the left side of the hip, with the fist –palm backward and the fist–hole down. Eyes look right forward.（Figure 33, Attached Figure 33）

圖 34

(2)上動不停。身體略向右轉，重心移至右腿；同時，左拳繼續向後、向上掄臂，拳心向下，拳眼向外，高與肩平；右前臂以肘關節為軸向前掄出，右拳以拳背向前砸拳，拳眼向右，高與眉齊；目視右拳。（圖 34）

(2)Keep the above action, turn the body to the right slightly, move the barycenter to the right leg. At the same time, swing the left arm backward and upward continuously, keep the fist−palm down and the fist−Plane outward at the shoulder height, swing the right forearm forward with the elbow joint as the pivot, smash with the right fist forward by the fist−back, with the fist−hole rightward at the eyebrow height. Eyes look at the right fist.（Figure 34）

七星螳螂拳　梅花路

圖 35

　　(3)上動不停。重心移至左腿，右腿提起向前點
腳；同時，左臂屈肘，向上擺架於頭左上方，拳心向
外，拳眼向前；右拳屈臂回收於胸前，拳心向裏，拳
面向上，高與肩平；目視右腳。（圖 35）

梅
花
路
套
路
動
作
圖
解

(3)Keep the above action, shift the barycenter to the left leg, raise the right one with toes on the ground forward. At the same, bend the left arm and parry it on the left part above the head with the fist–palm outward and the fist–hole forward, bend the right arm and draw back the right fist in front of the chest, with the fist–palm inward and the fist–plane at the shoulder height. Eyes look at the right foot. (Figure 35)

圖 36

16. 轉身回馬鞭　Turn body and whip backward

(1)接上勢。右腳向左腳左前方落步；同時，左拳向外、向下畫至右胯前，拳心向下，拳眼向裏；右拳經胸前上擺至頭頂，拳眼向下，拳心向前；目視右拳。（圖 36、圖 36 附圖）

圖 36 附圖

(1) Follow the above posture, the right foot falls to the left front of the left one. At the same time, swing the left fist outward and downward to the front of the right hip with the fist –palm down and the fist –hole inward. Swing the right fist upon the head top with the fist –hole down and the fist –palm forward. Eyes look at the right fist. ﹝ Figure 36, Attached figure 36 ﹞

圖 37

（2）上動不停。左腳向左側橫跨一步，右腳隨即跟步；左拳經胸前繼續上擺至右肩前，拳心向下，高與鼻齊；同時，右拳向外、向下擺至身右側，拳心向前，高與肩平；目視左拳。（圖 37、圖 37 附圖）

圖 37 附圖

(2) Keep the above action, the left foot strides a step to the left side, then the right one follows. Swing the left fist from the front of the chest to the front of the right shoulder with the fist – palm down at the nose height. At the same time, swing the right fist outward and downward to the right side of the body with the fist – palm forward at the shoulder height. Eyes look at the left fist. (Figure 37, Attached figure 37)

圖 38

(3)上動不停。身體向左轉 90°，下蹲成蹬山步；同時，兩拳直臂自右向左橫掃，拳心相對，高與肩平；右拳拳心向上，略低於左拳；目視前方。（圖 38）

(3) Keep the above action, turn the body 90° to the left, squat into mountaineering step. At the same time, the two fists sweep leftward horizontally with the arms straight, keep the two fist‑palms opposite at the shoulder level, keep the right fist‑palm up, slightly lower than the left fist. Eyes look forward.（Figure 38）

圖 39

第二段 Section Two

17. 右採迎面圈   Pick rightward for head-on circle

接上勢。身微右轉，重心移至右腿，左腳收回成左虛步；同時，左拳向右擺圈；右拳變掌，附於左前臂內側，掌指向上；目視左方。（圖 39）

Follow the above posture, slightly turn the body to the right, move the barycenter to the right leg, draw back the left foot into left empty stance. At the same time, swing the left fist rightward for a circle, change the right fist into palm and keep close to the inner side of the left forearm with the fingers up. Eyes look leftward.〔Figure 39〕

圖 40

18. 幫肘　Helping elbow

接上勢。身微左轉，左腳向前上步，隨即右腳向前跟步成蹬山步；同時，左拳屈臂向前推幫，拳心向下，拳輪向前，高與肩平；右掌心仍貼於左前臂內側，掌指向上；目視前方。（圖 40）

Follow the above posture, slightly turn the body to the left, the left foot takes forward, then the right one follows up into mountaineering step. At the same time, bend the left arm and push the left palm forward with the fist –palm down and the fist –wheel forward at the shoulder level, keep the right palm close to the inner side of the left forearm with the fingers up. Eyes look forward.（Figure 40）

圖 41

19. 七星拳　Seven-star fist

(1)接上勢。身體提起，重心移至左腿；同時，左拳變掌外旋向前探出，掌心向裏，掌指向前，高與肩平；右掌變拳，收抱於腰間，拳心向上；目視左掌。（圖 41）

(1) Follow the above posture, raise the body, shift the barycenter to the left leg. At the same time, change the left fist into palm and rotate it outward to stretch forward, keep the palm inward and the fingers forward at the shoulder height, change the right palm into fist, draw it back and hold on the waist with the fist-palm up. Eyes look at the left palm. (Figure 41)

圖 42

（2）上動不停。右腳向前上步，右腿蹬直，腳跟著地，左腿屈膝下蹲成七星步；同時，右拳向前平沖，拳心向下，拳眼向裏，高與肩平；左臂屈肘內旋，左掌迎擊右拳後掌心貼於右肘內側，掌指向上；目視右拳。（圖 42）

（2）Keep the above action, the right foot steps forward, the right leg straightens with the toes on ground, the left knee bends and squats into the seven-star stance. At the same time, the right fist punches forward horizontally, with the fist-palm down and fist-hole inward at the shoulder level, bend elbow of the left arm to whirl, the left palm counterpunches the right fist, then keep the palm close to the inner side of the right elbow with the fingers up. Eyes look at the right fist.（Figure 42）

梅花路套路動作圖解

圖 43

20. 左封右崩　Left wrap and right snap

(1)接上勢。右腳向前上半步，重心前移成右弓步；左臂屈肘，向前封抓變拳，拳心向下，高與肩平；右拳收抱於腰間，拳心向上。（圖 43）

(1) Follow the above posture, the right foot takes half–step forward, shift the barycenter forward into the right bow stance. The left arm bends the elbow and wrap forward into fist with the fist–palm down at the shoulder level, draw back the right fist and hold on the waist with the fist–center up.（Figure 43）

圖 44

(2)上動不停。右拳經左前臂內側向前崩拳，拳背向前，拳眼向右，高與鼻齊；同時，左拳屈肘回收，拳背貼於右肘下；目視右拳。（圖 44）

(2) Keep the above action, the right fist snaps punch forward through the inner side of the left forearm, with the fist–back forward and the fist–hole rightward at the nose level. At the same time, bend the left elbow to draw back the left fist, keep the fist–back sticking under the right elbow. Eyes look at the right fist.（Figure 44）

梅花路套路動作圖解

圖 45

21. 拉弓捶   Bow-pulling hammer

接上勢。左拳向左前方平沖，拳心向下，高與肩平；右前臂內旋，右拳回拉於右肩前，拳心向下，拳眼向裏；目視左拳。（圖 45）

Follow the above posture, the left fist strikes left forward horizontally, with the fist –palm down at the shoulder level, rotate the right forearm inward to draw back the right fist in front of the right shoulder with the fist –palm down and the fist –hole inward. Eyes look at the left fist.（Figure 45）

圖 46

22. 左採迎面圈　Pick leftward for head-on circle

接上勢。身體重心後移，左轉身 90°，右腳撤半步成右虛步；同時，右拳屈臂圈擺至胸前，拳心向下，拳面向左，高與肩平；左拳變掌，掌心貼於右肘內側，掌指向上；目視右方。（圖 46）

Follow the above posture, move the barycenter backward, turn the body 90° to the left, the right foot takes a half-step back into the right empty stance. At the same time, bend the right arm and swing for a circle to front of the chest, keep the fist-palm down and the fist-plane leftward at the shoulder height, change the left fist into palm and keep it close to the inner side of the right elbow with the fingers up. Eyes look rightward.（Figure 46）

圖 47

23. 幫肘　Helping elbow

接上勢。身微右轉，右腳向前上半步，隨即左腳
向前跟步成蹬山步；同時，右前臂內旋回收，高與肩
平；左掌心貼於右前臂內側向前推幫肘，掌心向前，
掌指向右；目視前方。（圖 47）

Follow the above posture, slightly turn the body to the right,
the right foot takes a half–step forward and follows up into the
mountaineering step. At the same time, whirl the right forearm
inward to draw back, at the shoulder height, keep the left palm
close to the inner side of the right forearm and push to help the
elbow forward with the palm forward and the fingers rightward.
Eyes look forward.〔Figure 47〕

圖 48

24. 二龍戲珠　Two dragons play pearl

（1）接上勢。右拳變掌，向前外摟手，掌心向前，虎口向下，高與肩平；左掌變拳，收抱於腰間，拳心向上；目視右掌。（圖 48）

（1）Follow the above posture, change the right fist into palm and grab outward, with the palm forward, the tiger´s mouth down, at the shoulder height. Change the left palm into fist, draw back and hold on the waist with the fist-palm up. Eyes look at the right palm.（Figure 48）

梅花路套路動作圖解

圖 49

(2)上動不停。左腳向前挪半步，身體右轉 90°成歇步；同時，右掌外摟變拳，收抱於腰間，拳心向上；左拳食指、中指分開前伸，成剪子手向前平插，手背向上，高與肩平；目視左手兩指。（圖 49）

(2) Keep the above action, the left foot takes a half–step forward, the body turns 90° to the right into the rest stance. At the same time, the right palm grabs outward and change it into fist, draw it back and hold on the waist with the fist–palm upward, part the forefinger and middle finger of the left fist and stretch forward into scissors hand and insert it forward horizontally with the back of the hand up at the shoulder height. Eyes look at two fingers of the left hand.（Figure 49）

圖50

25. 偸展磨盤打

Stretch secretly and the millstones strike

接上勢。身體提起，左腳向前上一步，隨即右腳跟半步，身體下蹲成蹬山步；同時，左手變掌，上托於頭左上方，隨即內旋下翻摟抓變拳向左拉帶，拳心向下，拳面向前，高與眼平；右拳變掌，向左前下方推掌至左膝外側，掌心向左，掌指向前；目視前方。（圖50）

Follow the above posture, the body lifts up, the left foot takes a step forward, then the right one follows a half–step, the body squats into mountaineering step. At the same time, change the left hand into palm and lift it to the left upper part of the head, then rotate inward, turn downward and grab into fist pull it leftward, keep the fist–palm down and the fist–plane forward at the eye level, change the right fist into palm and horizontally push it left–down forward to the outer side of the left knee with the palm leftward and the fingers forward. Eyes look forward. (Figure 50)

圖 51

26. 纏龍鎖口窩心腳　Intertwining dragon locks mouth and kicks toward heart

(1)接上勢。身體提起；同時，左拳收抱於腰間，拳心向上；右掌內旋，隨即外纏變為螳螂鉤，鉤尖向下，高與眉齊；目視前方。（圖 51）

(1) Follow the above posture, raise the body. At the same time, draw back the left fist and hold on the waist with the fist-palm up, rotate the right palm inward, then intertwine outward into mantis hook with the hook-tip down at the eyebrow height. Eyes look forward.（Figure 51）

梅花路套路動作圖解

圖 52

(2)上動不停。重心前移至左腿，右腿提起向前方蹬腳；同時，左拳變掌向前平推，掌心向前，掌指向上，高與肩平；右鉤手向後勾拉至右耳側，鉤尖向下；目視前方。（圖 52）

(2) Keep the above action, move the barycenter forward to the left leg, lift the right leg and kick forward with heel. At the same time, change the left fist into palm and push forward horizontally, with the palm forward and the fingers upward at the shoulder level, pull back the right hook hand to the side of the right ear with the hook –tip down. Eyes look forward. (Figure 52)

七星螳螂拳 梅花路

圖 53

27. 馬步劈砸
Hack and pound in horse stance

(1)接上勢。右腳向前落步；同時，右鉤手抓握變拳，拳心向下，拳面向右，置於右耳側；左掌外旋成掌指向前，掌心向裏，略低於肩；目視左掌。（圖 53）

梅
花
路
套
路
動
作
圖
解

(1)Follow the above posture, the right foot falls forward. At the same time, the right hook hand clenches into fist with the fist –palm down and the fist –plane rightward, place it at the side of the right ear, whirl the left palm outward, keep the fingers forward and the palm inward, lower than the shoulder slightly. Eyes look at the left palm. (Figure 53)

圖 54

(2)上動不停。身體左轉 90°，向下蹲身成馬步；同時，右拳隨轉身向前砸落於右膝前方，拳心向裏，拳輪向下；左掌向上迎擊右前臂內側，掌心貼於右肘關節，掌心向右，掌指向上；目視右拳。（圖 54）

(2) Keep the above action, turn the body 90° to the left, squat into horse stance. At the same time, the right fist punches forward with body turn and drops in front of the right knee with the fist –palm inward and the fist –wheel down, the left palm counterpunches the inner side of the right forearm upward, keep the palm close to the right elbow joint with the palm rightward and the fingers up. Eyes look at the right fist.（Figure 54）

圖 55

28. 左封右崩   Left wrap and right snap

(1)接上勢。身體右轉 90°成右弓步；同時，右拳收抱於腰間；左掌由外向裏封抓變拳，拳心向下，拳面向右，高與肩平；目視前方。（圖 55）

(1) Follow the above posture, turn the body 90° to the right into right bow stance. At the same time, draw back the right fist and hold on the waist, wrap the left palm inward from outside, change into fist, keep the fist –palm down and the fist –plane rightward at the shoulder height. Eyes look forward.（Figure 55）

圖 56

（2）上動不停。右拳經左前臂內側向前崩拳，拳面向上，拳眼向右，高與鼻齊；同時，左拳屈臂置於右肘下，拳心向下，拳面向右；目視前方。（圖 56）

（2）Keep the above action, the right fist snaps punch forward through the inner side of the left forearm, keep the fist-plane up and the fist-hole rightward at the nose height. At the same time, bend the left arm and place the left fist under the right elbow with the fist-palm down and the fist-plane rightward. Eyes look forward.〔Figure 56〕

梅花路套路動作圖解

圖 57

29. 轉身護眼指 Turn body and jab eyes

(1)接上勢。右拳經左臂內側收抱於腰間，拳心向上；同時，左前臂以肘關節為軸外旋格肘，左拳心向裏，拳眼向外，高與鼻齊；目視左拳。（圖 57）

(1) Follow the above posture, draw back the right fist through the inner side of the left arm and hold on the waist with the fist –palm up. At the same time, rotate the left forearm outward for elbow parry with the elbow joint as the axis, with the left fist –palm inward and the fist –hole outward at the nose level. Eyes look at the left fist.〔Figure 57〕

七星螳螂拳 梅花路

圖 58

　　(2)上動不停。身體左轉 180°，重心前移成左弓步；左臂繼續外旋格肘，左拳置於左耳側，拳心向後，拳眼向外；同時，右拳食、中兩指前伸成剪子手，隨轉身向前平插，手背向裏，高與肩平；身體微向左前方傾斜；目視兩指。（圖 58、圖 58 附圖）

圖 58 附圖

(2) Keep the above action, turn the body 180° to the left, shift the barycenter forward into left bow stance. The left arm rotates outward continuously, place the place the left fist on the outside of the left ear, with fist－palm backward and fist－hole outward. At the same time, the forefinger and middle finger of the right fist stretch forward into scissors hand, inserts forward horizontally with body turn, keep the back of the hand inward at the shoulder height. Slightly slant the body left forward. Eyes look at the two fingers. (Figure 58, Attached figure 58)

圖 59

30. 螳螂雙封手　Mantis closes up hands

（1）接上勢。身體重心後移；同時，兩手變掌，右掌向胸前屈臂回收；左掌向右下方插掌，與右前臂相交於腹前，兩掌掌心均向下；目視兩掌。（圖 59）

(1) Follow the above posture, shift the barycenter back. At the same time, change the two hands into palms, bend the arm to draw back the right palm to the front of the chest, the left palm inserts right downward and crosses with the right forearm in front of the abdomen, with the two palms down. Eyes look at the two palms.（Figure 59）

圖 60

　(2)上動不停。身體略向後傾斜；同時，兩臂屈肘，兩掌在胸前翻轉絞手，右掌心向上，掌指向右；左掌心向右，掌指向後，高與頜平；目視兩掌。（圖60）

　(2) Keep the above action, slightly slant the body backward. At the same time, bend the elbows of two arms and turn over and twist the two palms in front of the chest, with the right palm up and the fingers rightward, keep the left palm leftward and the fingers backward at the chin height. Eyes look at the two palms. 〔Figure 60〕

圖 61

　　(3)上動不停。重心略前移；同時，右掌前探，虎口向上，掌心向前，高與肩平；左掌護於右肩前，掌心向右，掌指向後；目視右掌。（圖 61）

　　(3) Keep the above action, shift the barycenter forward slightly. At the same time, the right palm stretches forward, with the tiger´s mouth up and the palm forward at the shoulder height, the left palm guards in front of the right shoulder with the palm rightward and the fingers backward. Eyes look at the right palm.（Figure 61）

圖 62

(4)上動不停。右臂屈肘，右掌變為螳螂鉤，吊腕回拉於胸前，鉤尖向下；同時，左掌前伸成掌指向右，掌心向前，高與肩平；目視左掌。（圖 62）

(4) Keep the above action, bend the right elbow, change the right palm into mantis hook and hang the wrist and draw back to the front of the chest with the hook–tip down. At the same time, the left palm stretches forward with the fingers rightward and the palm forward at the shoulder height. Eyes look at the left palm. 〔 Figure 62 〕

圖 63

(5)上動不停。左腳向後退半步，重心後移成左虛步；同時，左臂屈肘，左掌變為螳螂鈎，吊腕回拉於左膝上方，鈎尖向前，高與肩平；目視前方。（圖63）

(5) Keep the above action, the left foot takes a half-step backward, shift the barycenter backward into left empty stance. At the same time, bend the left elbow, change the left palm into mantis hook, hang the wrist and draw back upon the left knee with the hook-tip forward at the shoulder height. Eyes look forward.〔 Figure 63 〕

圖 64

第三段　Section Three

31. 左右護腿　Guard left and right legs

（1）接上勢。身體提起，微向右轉；同時，兩鉤手變拳，右拳收抱於腰間，拳心向上；左臂屈肘擺至右胸前，左拳心向後，略高於肩；目視左下方。（圖 64）

（1）Follow the above posture, raise the body and slightly turn to the right. At the same time, change the two hook hands into fists, draw back the right fist and hold on the waist with the fist－palm upward, bend the left elbow and swing to the front of the right chest with the left fist－palm backward, slightly higher than the shoulder. Eyes look left downward.〔Figure 64〕

圖 65

（2）上動不停。右腿獨立，左膝提起，腳尖內扣；
同時，左拳經左膝外側向下、向後格擊，拳眼向前，
拳心向下；目視左拳。（圖 65）

（2）Keep the above action, the left leg stands alone, the left
knee lifts up with toes turning inward. At the same time, parry
the left fist downward and backward through the outer side of
the left knee with the fist–hole forward and the fist–palm down.
Eyes look at the left fist.〔Figure 65〕

圖66

(3)上動不停。身體左轉180°，左腳向左前方落步；同時，左拳收抱於腰間；右拳屈臂，向上抬至右耳側，拳心向裏，拳眼向後；目視右下方。（圖66）

(3) Keep the above action, turn the body to the left by 180°, the left foot lands left forward. At the same time, draw the left fist back and hold on the waist; bend the right arm and lift the right fist to the side of the right ear with the fist–palm inward and the fist–hole backward. Eyes look right downward. 〔Figure 66〕

圖 67

(4)上動不停。左腿獨立，右腿提起，腳尖內扣；
同時，右拳經右膝外側向下、向後格擊，拳眼向前，
拳心向裏；目視右拳。（圖67）

(4) Keep the above action, the left leg stands alone, the right
leg lifts up with toes turning inward. At the same time, parry the
with right fist downward and backward through the outer side of
the right knee with the fist –hole forward and the fist –palm
inward. Eyes look at the right fist.〔Figure 67〕

圖 68

32. 起身貫耳　Rise body to strike ears

接上勢。左腳蹬地跳起；同時，右拳掄臂向前、
向裏貫擊，拳面向左，拳眼向下，高與頭頂平；左拳
變掌，向裏迎擊右前臂，掌心貼於右前臂內側，掌指
向上；目視前方。（圖 68）

Follow the above posture, the left foot press against ground
to jump up. At the same time, swing the right fist forward and
inward for striking, with the fist –plane leftward and the fist –
hole down at the head top level; change the left fist into palm
and counterpunch the right forearm, keep the palm close to the
inner side of the right forearm and the fingers up. Eyes look
forward.（Figure 68）

圖 69

33. 落地下掃襠
Land on ground to sweep crotch

接上勢。兩腳右前左後落地，身體下蹲成蹬山步。同時，右拳隨身體下落在腰前圈捶擊，拳心向下，拳面向右，高與膝平。左掌向裏迎擊右前臂，掌心貼於右前臂內側，掌指向後；目視右拳。（圖 69、圖 69 附圖）

圖 69 附圖

Follow the above posture, the feet fall to the ground right forward and left backward, the body squats into mountaineering step. At the same time, the right fist falls with the body circle hammar before slomach keep the fist –palm downward and the fist –plane rightward at the knee level.   The left palm counterpunches the right forearm inward with the palm close to the inner side of the right forearm and the fingers backward. Eyes look at the right fist. 〔Figure 69, Attached figure 69〕

圖 70

34. 進步打中堂　Step forward to strike Zhongtang

接上勢。右腳向前上一步，左腳隨即跟半步，仍成蹬山步；同時，右拳在體前圈捶擊，拳面向右，拳眼向下，高與肩平；左掌向裏迎擊，掌心貼於右前臂，掌指向上；目視前方。（圖 70）

Follow the above posture, the right foot takes a step forward, then the left one follows a half–step into mountaineering step. At the same time, the right fist circle hammer before the body, with the fist–plane of the fist rightward and the fist–hole down at the shoulder height, the left palm counterpunches inward, keep the palm close to the right forearm, with the fingers up. Eyes look forward.（Figure 70）

圖71

35. 採手右崩點　Pick hand and snap point

(1)接上勢。身體提起，重心移至右腳；同時，右拳變掌外翻，成掌心向下，虎口向裏，高與肩平；目視右掌。（圖71）

(1) Follow the above posture, raise the body, move the barycenter to the right foot. At the same time, change the right fist into palm and turn it outward, with the palm down, the tiger's mouth inward, at the shoulder height. Eyes look at the right palm.（Figure 71）

圖 72

(2)上動不停。右手抓握變拳，收抱於腰間，拳心向上；同時，左掌向前封抓變拳，拳心向下，拳面向右，高與肩平；目視左拳。（圖 72）

(2) Keep the above action, the right hand clenches into fist, draw it back and hold on the waist with the fist−palm up. At the same time, change the left palm into fist and grab forward into fist, with the fist−palm down and the fist−plane ightward at the shoulder height. Eyes look at the left fist.〔Figure 72〕

梅花路套路動作圖解

圖 73

(3)上動不停。身略左轉；同時，左拳屈臂回收；
右拳經左前臂內側以拳背向前崩點，拳面向上，拳眼
向右；左拳背貼於右肘下，拳面向右；目視前方。
（圖 73）

(3) Keep the above action, slightly turn the body to the left.
At the same time, bend the left arm to draw back the left fist, the
right fist snaps punch forward through the inner side of the left
forearm with the fist–plane up and the fist–hole ightward. Keep
the left fist sticking under the right elbow with the fist –plane
rightward. Eyes look forward.（Figure 73）

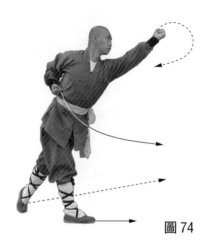

圖 74

36. 偷展磨盤打
Stretch secretly and millstones strike

(1)接上勢。身體略向右轉 45°成叉步；同時，右拳收抱於腰間，拳心向上；左拳經右臂外側向前上方沖拳，拳心向上；目視左拳。（圖 74）

(1) Follow the above posture, slightly turn the body 45° to the right into cross stance. At the same time, draw back the right fist and hold on the waist with the fist –palm up, the left fist strikes upward ahead through the outer side of the right arm, with the fist –palm up and the fist –hole outward at the head height. Eyes look at the left fist. (Figure 74)

圖 75

(2)上動不停。左腳向前上一步，右腳隨即跟步，身體下蹲成玉環步；同時，左拳裏旋外擺於頭左前方，拳眼向右，拳面向前，高與眉齊；右拳經胸前向左膝前方沖拳，拳眼向上；目視前方。（圖 75）

(2) Keep the above action, the left foot takes a step forward, then the right one follows up, the body squats into the jade-ring step. At the same time, rotate the left fist inward and swing outward to the left front of the head, keep the fist-hole rightward and the fist-plane forward at the eyebrow height; the right fist strikes to the front of the left knee through the front of the chest with the fist-hole up. Eyes look forward. (Figure 75)

圖 76

37. 轉身左封右崩
Left wrap and right snap with body turn

(1)接上勢。身體右轉 180°，重心移至左腿，身體提起，右膝提起，腳尖內扣；同時，右拳隨轉身收抱於腰間，拳心向上；左掌向胸前畫弧裏擺，掌心向前，掌指向右，高與肩平；目視左掌。（圖 76）

梅花路套路動作圖解

(1)Follow the above posture, turn the body 180° to the right, move the barycenter to the left leg, raise the body and lift the right knee with toes turning inward. At the same time, draw back the right fist and hold on the waist with the fist−palm up; swing the left palm inward through the front of the chest to draw a curve with the palm forward and the fingers rightward at the shoulder height. Eyes look at the left palm. (Figure 76)

圖 77

　　(2)上動不停。右腳向前落步，左腳隨即跟步，身體下蹲成蹬山步；左掌抓握變拳，屈臂回收於胸前，前臂與上臂垂直，拳心向下；右拳拳心向裏，經左前臂內側向前崩拳，屈臂置於胸前，拳心向裏，拳面向上，高與頜平；左拳背貼於右肘下，拳面向左；目視前方。（圖77）

梅
花
路
套
路
動
作
圖
解

(2) Keep the above action, the right foot falls forward, then the left one follows up, the body squats into mountaineering stance. Clench the left palm into fist, bend the arm to draw back to the front of the chest, the forearm and the upper part of the arm shall be upright with the fist-palm down, the right fist snaps punch forward through the inner side of the left forearm with the fist-palm inward, bend the arm and place it in front of the chest, with the fist-palm inward and the fist-plane of the fist up at the chin height. The left fist back attaches to the downward of the right elbow, with fist-plane of the fist rightward. (Figure 77)

圖 78

38. 叫手擒摔
Call hands for capturing throw

(1)接上勢。身體向上提起；同時，兩拳變掌，右臂內旋，成掌心向下，虎口向裏，高與肩平；左掌前伸外旋，成掌心向上，掌指向前，略低於右掌；目視兩掌。（圖 78）

梅花路套路動作圖解

(1) Follow the above posture, raise the body. At the same time, change the two fists into palms, whirl the right arm inward, keep the palm down, the tiger´s mouth inward, at the shoulder height, the left palm stretches forward and rotate it outward, keep the palm upward and the fingers forward, slightly lower than the right one. Eyes look at the two palms. (Figure 78)

圖 79

(2)上動不停。左腿微屈膝，重心後移至左腿；兩手抓握變拳，向右側回拉，右拳拳心向下，拳眼向前，高與肩平；左拳拳心向上，略低於右肩；目視右拳。（圖 79、圖 79 附圖）

要點：此式意在擒摔，擰腰回帶要迅猛有力。

梅花路套路動作圖解

圖 79 附圖

(2) Keep the above action, bend the left leg slightly, move the barycenter backward to the left leg. The two hands clench into fists and draw back rightward. keep the right fist −palm down, the fist −hole forward at the shoulder level, for the left one, the fist−palm shall be upward, slightly lower than the right shoulder. Eyes look at the right fist. ﹝ Figure 79, Attached figure79 ﹞

Key points: This form intends to capture and wrestle, twisting the waist and drawing back shall be swift and forceful.

圖80

39. 左封右圈捶
Left wrap and right circular hammar

接上勢。右腳向前上一步，隨即左腳跟步，蹲身成蹬山步；同時，右拳向前、向裏圈擊，拳面向左，拳心向下，高與肩平；左拳變掌，向左畫弧，隨即向裏迎擊右前臂，掌心貼於右前臂內側，掌指向上；目視右拳。（圖80）

梅
花
路
套
路
動
作
圖
解

Follow the above posture, the right foot takes a step forward, then the left one follows up, the body squats into mountaineering step. At the same time, the right fist strikes forward and inward circularly, with the fist–plane leftward and the fist–palm down at the shoulder height; change the left fist into palm and draw a curve leftward, then counterpunch the right forearm inward, keep the palm close to the inner side of the right forearm with the fingers up. Eyes look at the right fist. (Figure 80)

圖 81

40. 鳳凰三點頭　Phoenix nods three times

(1)接上勢。左腿蹬直，重心前移成右弓步；同時，右拳變掌外摟，掌心向前，掌指向上，高與肩平；左掌變拳，收抱於腰間，拳心向上；目視右掌。（圖 81）

(1) Follow the above posture, the left leg straightens, shift the barycenter forward into right bow stance. At the same time, change the right fist into palm and grab outward, with the palm forward and the fingers up, at the shoulder level; change the left palm into fist, draw it back and hold on the waist with the fist – palm up. Eyes look at the right palm.（Figure 81.）

圖 82

(2)上動不停。右手變拳，收抱於腰間；左拳向前平沖，拳心向下，高與肩平；目視左拳。（圖 82）

(2)Keep the above action, change the right hand into fist, draw it back and hold on the waist, the left fist strikes forward horizontally with the fist –palm down at the shoulder height. Eyes look at the left fist.（Figure 82）

圖 83

（3）上動不停。左拳收抱於腰間，拳心向上；右拳
向前平沖，拳心向下，高與肩平；目視右拳。（圖
83）

（3）Keep the above action, draw the left fist back and hold on
the waist with the fist－palm up; the right fist strikes forward
horizontally with the fist－palm downward at the shoulder height.
Eyes look at the right fist.〔Figure 83〕

梅花路套路動作圖解

圖 84

(4)上動不停。右拳收抱於腰間，拳心向上；左拳向前平沖，拳心向下，高與肩平；目視左拳。（圖84）

(4) Keep the above action, draw the right fist back and hold on the waist with the fist－Palm up; the left fist strikes forward horizontally with the fist－palm down at the shoulder height. Eyes look at the left fist.〔Figure 84〕

圖 85

41. 臨行鴛鴦腳
Mandarin-duck foot before leaving

(1)接上勢。左轉身 90°，重心移至兩腿間；同時，左拳隨身向下、向後擺拳，拳眼向下；右臂內旋裏擺於胸前，右拳置於左肩前，拳眼向裏，拳心向下；目視右方。（圖 85）

(1)Follow the above posture, the body turns 90°to the left and transfer the barycenter between two legs. At the same time, the left fist swings downward and backward, with the fist–hole down, rotate the right arm and swing before the chest, put the right fist before the left shoulder, with the fist–hole inward and the fist–palm down. Eyes look rightward.（Figure 85）

梅花路套路動作圖解

圖 86

(2)上動不停。身體略向右轉；同時，左拳繼續向上擺拳，拳心向下，拳眼向前，高與肩平；掄右臂，右拳向前反砸，拳心向上，高與肩平；目視右拳。（圖 86）

(2) Keep the above action, the body turns to the right slightly. At the same time, the left fist swings upward, with the fist −palm down and the fist −hole forward at the shoulder height, swing the right arm and right fist forward for back pounding, with the fist −palm up at the shoulder height. Eyes look at the right fist.〔Figure 86〕

圖 87

(3)上動不停。重心後移至左腿，右腿抬起向前彈踢；同時，右拳屈臂回收於胸前，拳心向裏，置於右膝內側上方；左拳屈臂上擺於頭右上方，拳心向外；目視右拳。（圖 87）

梅花路套路動作圖解

(3) Keep the above action, transfer the barycenter backward onto the left leg, lift the right one for snap kick forward. At the same time, bend the right arm and draw back the right fist before the chest, with the fist–palm inward and putting above the inner side of the right knee, bend the left arm and swing the left fist right overhead, with the fist –palm outward. Eyes look at the right fist. ﹝Figure 87﹞

圖 88

42. 雙幫肘　Double helping elbows

(1)接上勢。右腳收回不落地，成左獨立勢；同時，左拳向下、右拳向上抱拳於胸前，右拳在外，左拳在裏，兩拳心均向下，拳眼均向裏，高與肩平；目視兩拳。（圖 88）

(1)Follow the above posture, draw back the right foot not to fall to the ground and stand on left one. At the same time, hold the fists before the chest with the left one downward and right one on top, the right one outward and the left one inward, the fist–palms down and the fist–holes inward at the shoulder level. Eyes look at the fists.（Figure 88）

梅花路套路動作圖解

圖 89

　(2)上動不停。右腳向前落步，左腳隨即跟步成蹬山步；兩臂同時向前推幫肘，兩拳心向下，高與肩平；目視前方。（圖89）

　(2) Keep the above action, the right foot falls forward, then the left one follows up into the mountaineering step. Push forward with both elbows, with the fist −palms down at the shoulder height. Eyes look forward. 〔Figure 89〕

圖 90

第四段　Section Four

43. 退步翻車　Step back and turn over

(1)接上勢。起身，略向右轉身；同時，右臂向下、向後掄擺，拳心向下，高與肩平；目視左拳。（圖 90）

(1) Follow the above posture, the body stands up and turns to the right slightly. At the same time, the right arm swings downward and backward, with the fist –palm down at the shoulder height. Eyes look at the left fist. (Figure 90)

圖 91

(2)上動不停。右腳向後撤一步，身體左轉 90°成叉步；同時，右臂從後向上、向前掄臂砸拳；左臂向下、向後掄臂，兩拳眼均向上，拳心均向前，高與肩平；目視右拳。（圖 91）

(2) Keep the above action, the right foot takes a step back, the body turns 90° to the left to change into the cross stance. At the same time, the right arm swings upward and forward from back for pounding; the left arm swings downward and backward, with the fist –holes up and the fist –palms forward at the shoulder height. Eyes look at the right fist.〔Figure 91〕

圖 92

（3）上動不停。左腳向後撤一步，身體向右轉 90°；同時，左臂向上、向前掄臂砸拳，拳眼向上，拳心向裏；右臂向下、向後掄臂，拳眼向下，拳背向外，兩臂高與肩平；目視左拳。（圖 92）

(3) Keep the above action, the left foot takes a step back and the body turns 90° to the right. At the same time, the left arm swings upward and forward for pounding, with the fist–hole up and the fist–palm inward; the right arm swings downward and backward, with the fist–hole down and the fist–back outward. Keep the arms high with the shoulders. Eyes look at the left fist. 〔Figure 92〕

圖 93

(4)上動不停。右腳向後撤一步，身體左轉 90°成叉步；同時，右臂向上、向前掄臂砸拳；左臂向下、向後掄臂，兩拳眼均向上，拳心均向前，高與肩平；目視右拳。（圖 93）

(4) Keep the above action, the right foot takes a step back and the body turns 90° to the left by to change into the cross stance. At the same time, the right arm swings up and forward for pounding; the left arm swings downward and backward, with the fist –holes up and the fist –palms forward at the shoulder height. Eyes look at the right fist.（Figure 93）

圖 94

（5）上動不停。左腳向後撤一步，身體向右轉 90°；同時，左臂向上、向前掄臂砸拳，拳眼向上，拳心向裏；右臂向下、向後掄臂，拳眼向下，拳背向外，兩臂高與肩平；目視左拳。（圖 94）

（5）Keep the above action, the left foot takes a step back and the body turns 90° to the right. At the same time, the left arm swings upward and forward for pounding, with the left fist–hole up and the fist –palm inward; the right arm swings downward and backward, with the right fist–hole down and the fist–back outward. Keep the arms at the shoulders height. Eyes look at the left fist.（Figure 94）

圖 95

(6)上動不停。身體左轉 90°；同時，右臂向上、向前掄臂砸拳；左臂向下、向後掄臂，兩拳眼均向上，拳心均向前，高與肩平；目視右拳。（圖 95）

(6)Keep the above action, the body turns 90° to the left. At the same time, right arm swing upward and forward for pounding; the left arm swings downward and backward, with the fist−holes up and the fist−palm forward at the shoulder height. Eyes look at the right fist.（Figure 95）

圖 96

　　(7)上動不停。身體右轉 45°，右腳抬起向前蹬
伸，腳尖上勾，左腿屈膝下蹲成七星步；同時，左拳
向上擺架於頭左上方，左臂微屈，拳心向裏，拳眼向
後；右拳向下、向後擺於身右側，拳心向下，拳眼向
前，略高於胯；目視右方。（圖 96、圖 96 附圖）

梅花路套路動作圖解

圖 96 附圖

(7) Keep the above action, the body turns 45° to the right, the right foot lifts forward for kicking with the tiptces hooking up, bend the knee of the left leg and squat into the seven-star stance. At the same time, parry upward with left fist left overhead, bend the left arm slightly, with the fist-palm inward and the fist-hole backward. The right fist swings downward and backward at the right of the Body, with the fist-palm down and the fist-hole forward, higher than the hip slightly. Eyes look rightward.〔 Figure 96, Attached figure 96 〕

圖 97

44. 進步轆轤靠
Step forward and lean with windlass

（1）接上勢。身體右轉 45°，左腿獨立，右腳抬起；同時，右拳繼續向後、向上擺，拳眼向下，高與肩平；左拳變掌，向前、向下畫掌，掌心向裏，掌指向前，高與肩平；目視前方。（圖 97）

(1) Follow the above posture, the body turns 45° to the right, the left leg stands alone and the right foot lift up. At the same time, swing the right fist backward and upward, with the fist – hole down at the shoulder height; change the left fist into palm to pull forward and downward, with the palm inward and the fingers forward at the shoulder height. Eyes look forward. （Figure 97）

圖 98

(2)上動不停。右腳向前落步，左腳隨即跟步；同時，右臂從後向前、向上掄擊，拳心向裏，拳眼向上，高與肩平；左掌向裏、向下迎擊右前臂，掌指向上，掌心貼於右前臂內側；目視右拳。（圖 98）

(2) Keep the above action, the right foot falls forward, the left one follows up. At the same time, the right arm swings forward and upward from back, with the fist–palm inward and the fist hole up at the shoulder level; the left palm unterpunches the right forearm inward and downward, with the fingers up and the palm sticking to the inner side of the right forearm. Eyes look at the right fist.〔Figure 98〕

圖 99

（3）上動不停。身體略向右轉，右腿向上抬起；同時，右臂繼續向上、向後掄掃，拳眼向下；左掌向下、向前畫掌，掌心向裏，掌指向前；目視前方。（圖99）

(3) Keep the above action, the body turns to the right slightly, the right leg lifts up. At the same time, the right arm sweeps upward and backward, with the fist－hole down, the left palm pulls downward and forward, with the palm inward and the fingers forward. Eyes look forward.（Figure 99）

梅花路套路動作圖解

圖 100

　　(4)上動不停。右腳向前落步，左腳隨即跟步；同時，右臂從後向前、向上掄擊，右拳拳心向裏，拳眼向上，高與肩平；左掌向裏、向下迎擊右前臂，掌指向上，掌心貼於右前臂內側；目視右拳。（圖 100）

　　(4) Keep the above action, the right foot lands forward, then the left one follows up. At the same time, the right arm swings forward and upward, with the right fist –palm inward and the fist–hole up at the shoulder height; the left palm counterpunches the right forearm inward and downward, with the fingers up and the palm sticking to the inner side of the right forearm. Eyes look at the right fist.〔Figure 100〕

圖 101

（5）上動不停。身體略向右轉，右腿向上抬起；同時，右臂繼續向上、向後掄臂，拳眼向下；左掌向下、向前畫掌，掌心向裏，掌指向前；目視前方。（圖101）

（5）Keep the above action, the body turns to the right slightly and the right leg lift up. At the same time, the right arm swings upward and backward, with the fist –hole downward; the left palm pulls downward and forward, with the palm inward and the fingers forward. Eyes look forward.（Figure 101）

梅花路套路動作圖解

圖 102

(6)上動不停。右腳向前落步，左腳隨即跟步；同時，右臂從後向前、向上掄擊，拳心向裏，拳眼向上，高與肩平；左掌向裏、向下迎擊右前臂，掌指向上，掌心貼於右前臂內側；目視右拳。（圖 102）

(6)Keep the above action, the right foot lands forward, then the left one follows up. At the same time, the right arm swings forward and upward, with the fist –palm inward and the palm hole upward at the shoulder level; the left palm counterpunches the right forearm inward and downward, with the fingers up and the palm sticking to the inner side of the right forearm. Eyes look at the right fist.〔Figure 102〕

圖 103

（7）上動不停。身體略向右轉，右腿向上抬起；同時，右臂繼續向上、向後掄臂，拳眼向下；左掌向下、向前畫掌，掌心向裏，掌指向前，兩臂處於同一水平；目視前方。（圖 103）

(7)Keep the above action, the body turns to the right slightly and the right leg lifts up. At the same time, the right arm swings upward and backward, with the fist-hole down, the left palm pulls downward and forward, with the palm inward and the fingers forward. Keep the arms at the same level. Eyes look forward.（Figure 103）

圖 104

(8)上動不停。右腳向前落步，左腳隨即跟步；同時，右臂從後向前、向上掄擊，拳心向裏，拳眼向上，高與肩平；左掌向裏、向下迎擊右前臂，掌指向上，掌心貼於右前臂內側；目視右拳。（圖 104）

(8) Keep the above action, the right foot lands forward, then the left one follows up. At the same time, the right arm swings forward and upward from the back, with the fist–palm inward and the fist–hole up at the shoulder height; the left palm counterpunches the right forearm inward and downward, with the fingers up and the palm sticking to the inner side of the right forearm. Eyes look at the right fist.〔Figure 104〕

圖 105

45. 左封右陽拳　Left wrap and right Yang fist

（1）接上勢。身體略向右轉，右腿蹬直向上抬起；同時，右臂向上、向後掄臂，右拳收抱於腰間；左掌向下、向前擺掌，掌心向裏，掌指向前，高與肩平；目視左掌。（圖 105）

（1）Follow the above action, the body turns to the right slightly, the right leg kicks straight to lift up. At the same time, swing the right arm upward and backward, draw back the right fist and hold on the waist; swing the left palm downward and forward, with the palm inward and the fingers forward at the shoulder height. Eyes look at the left palm.（Figure 105）

圖106

（2）上動不停。重心前移，右腳向前上步，左腳隨
即跟步；同時，左臂屈肘收回，左掌變拳收於胸前；
右拳經左前臂內側向上沖拳，拳心向上，拳眼向外，
高與眉齊；左拳眼向裏，拳背貼於右肘下；目視右
拳。（圖106）

(2) Keep the above action, transfer the barycenter forward,
the right foot steps forward, then the left one follows up. At the
same time, bend elbow of the left arm and draw it back, change
the left palm into fist and draw it back before the chest; the right
fist strikes upward through the inner side of the left forearm,
with the fist–palm up and the fist–hole outward at the eyebrow
level; the left fist–hole inward, sticking the fits–back under the
right elbow. Eyes look at the right fist.〔Figure 106〕

圖 107

(3)上動不停。身體下蹲成蹬山步；兩臂肘同時略微下沉，右拳心向裏，拳面向上，高與頜平；目視右拳。（圖 107）

(3) Keep the above action, the body squats into the mountaineering step. Elbows of two arms sink simultaneously, with the right fist–palm inward and the fist–plane up at the chin height. Eyes look at the right fist.〔 Figure 107 〕

圖 108

46. 雙分左格肘
Double parting and parrying with left elbow

(1)接上勢。身體提起，右腳向身右側撤一步，兩腳開立，與肩同寬；同時，兩拳經胸前上舉於頭頂，隨即向兩側分拳，兩臂伸直成水平，兩拳拳心均向前，拳眼均向上；目視前方。（圖108）

(1) Follow the above action, the body raises, the right foot takes a step back rightward, two feet stand for the shoulder-width apart. At the same time, lift the hands overhead through the front of the chest, then part the fists to both sides, two arms stretch straight to be horizontal, with the fist-palms forward and the fist-holes up. Eyes look forward.〔Figure 108〕

圖 109

　　(2)上動不停。左腳向右腳前上一步，腳跟著地，身體下蹲成七星步；同時，右臂屈肘收於胸前，拳面向左，拳心向下；左拳向下畫弧，經胸前向外格肘，拳心向裏，拳眼向左，高與頜平；右拳背貼於左肘下；目視左方。（圖 109）

梅
花
路
套
路
動
作
圖
解

(2) Keep the above action, the left foot takes a step forward to the right one with the heel on the ground, the body squats into the seven-star stance. At the same time, bend elbow of the right arm and draw back before the chest, with the fist-plane leftward and the fist-palm down, the left palm draws a curve downward for outward parry elbow through the front of the chest, with the fist-palm inward and the fist-hole leftward at the chin heigh. Stick the right fist under the left elbow. Eyes look leftward. (Figure 109)

圖 110

47. 雙分右格肘
Double parting and parrying with right elbow

（1）接上勢。身體提起，左腳向身左側撤一步，兩腳開立，與肩同寬；同時，兩拳經胸前舉於頭頂，隨即向兩側分拳，兩臂伸直成水平，兩拳拳心均向前，拳眼均向上；目視前方。（圖110）

（1）Follow the above posture, uplift the body, the left foot takes a step back leftward, two feet stand for the shoulder-width apart. At the same time, lift the fists overhead through the front of the chest, then part the fists to both sides, two arms stretch straight to be horizontal, with the fist-palms forward and the fist-holes up. Eyes look forward.（Figure 110）

圖 111

(2)上動不停。右腳向左腳前上一步，腳跟著地，身體下蹲成七星步；同時，左臂屈肘收於胸前，拳面向左，拳心向下；右拳下畫經胸前向外格肘，拳心向裏，拳眼向右，高與頜平，左拳背貼於右肘下；目視右方。（圖 111）

(2)Keep the above action, the right foot takes a step forward to the front of the left one with the heel on the ground. The body squats into the seven–star stance. At the same time, bend elbow of the left arm and draw back before the chest, with the fist – plane leftward and the fist–palm down; the right fist pull down for outward parry elbow through the front of the chest, with the fist–Palm inward and the fist–hole rightward at the chin height. Stick the left fist –back under the right elbow. Eyes look rightward.（Figure 111）

圖 112

48. 左擒右蹬踏
Left capture and right stamp

(1)接上勢。身體左轉 90°，重心移至右腳，隨即左腳向右腿後插步；兩拳變掌，右掌畫弧裏擺，與左掌交叉於胸前，右掌掌心向右，掌指向前；左掌掌心向下，虎口向裏，置於右肘下；目視右掌。（圖 112）

梅
花
路
套
路
動
作
圖
解

(1) Follow the above posture, the body turns 90° to the left, transfer the barycenter to the right foot, then the left foot does back cross step to the right leg. Change two fists into palms, the right palm draws a curve and swings inward, cross before the chest with the left palm, with the right palm rightward, the fingers forward; the left palm down, tiger´s mouth inward and put under the right elbow. Eyes look at the right palm. (Figure 112)

圖113

（2）上動不停。右腿向前伸直；同時，右掌向後擺掌，虎口向外，掌指向後；左掌變拳向前擺，拳心向外，拳眼向下，高與肩平；目視右腳。（圖113）

(2) Keep the above action, the right leg stretches forward straight. At the same time, the right palm swings backward, with tiger´s mouth outward and the fingers backward, change the left palm into fist to swing forward, with the fist—palm outward and the fist—hole down at the shoulder height. Eyes look at the right foot.（Figure 113）

梅花路套路動作圖解

圖 114

(3)上動不停。身體略向左轉，右腿向右後方蹬踢
地面落地，身略前傾成左弓步；同時，左拳收抱於腰
間；右掌向身體右前方撩推掌，掌心向前，掌指向斜
下方，高與左膝平；目視右掌。（圖 114）

(3)Keep the above action, the body turns to the left slightly,
the right leg kicks right backward and lands to the ground, the
body slants forward slightly to change into the left bow stance.
At the same time, draw back the left fist and hold on the waist,
the right palm raises and pushes right ahead of the body, with the
palm forward and the fingers down aslant at the left knee height.
Eyes look at the right palm. ﹝Figure 114﹞

圖 115

49. 反掌擊面　 Turn over palm to hit face

接上勢。身體略向右轉；同時，右掌反掌向右上方擺擊，掌背向後，掌指向斜上方，高與頭頂平；目視右掌。（圖 115）

Follow the above posture, the body turns to the right slightly. At the same time, turn over the right palm to swing and punch right upward, with the palm back backward and the fingers up aslant at the head top level. Eyes look at the right palm. ﹝ Figure 115﹞

圖 116

50. 雙分左閉手
Double parting and left hand close‑up

(1)接上勢。起身向右轉 90°，右腳向右側撤一步，兩腳開立，與肩同寬；同時，左拳變掌，兩掌交叉，經胸前向上托舉於頭頂上方，隨即向兩側分掌，兩掌心向外，掌指均向上，兩臂成水平；目視前方。（圖 116）

(1) Follow the above posture, the body stands up and turns 90° to the right, the right foot takes a step rightward, the feet stand for the shoulder‑width apart. At the same time, change the left fist into palm, cross the palms to lift overhead through the front of the chest, then part the palms to both sides, with the palms outward and the fingers up. Keep the arms horizontal. Eyes look forward. (Figure 116)

圖 117

　　(2)上動不停。身體略向右轉，左腳向右腳前方上
一步，腳跟著地，身體下蹲成七星步；同時，左掌向
裏畫弧，經胸前再向上、向外畫掌，掌心向前，掌指
向上，高與肩平；右掌向裏畫弧，立掌於左肘內側下
方，掌心向左，掌指向上；目視左掌。（圖117）

梅花路套路動作圖解

(2) Keep the above action, the body turns to the right slightly, the left foot takes a step to the front of the right one with the heel on the ground, the body squats into the seven – star stance. At the same time, the left palm draws a curve inward, then draw upward and outward through the front of the chest, with the palm forward and the fingers up at the shoulder level; the right palm draws a curve inward under the inner side of the left elbow with the standing palm, with the palm leftward and the fingers up. Eyes look the left palm. (Figure 117)

圖 118

51. 雙分右閉手
Double parting and right hand close-up

　　(1)接上勢。起身向左轉 45°，左腳向左側撤一步，兩腳開立，與肩同寬；同時，兩掌交叉，經胸前向上托舉於頭頂上方，隨即向兩側分掌，兩掌心向外，掌指均向上，兩臂成水平；目視前方。（圖 118）

梅花路套路動作圖解

(1) Follow the above posture, the body stands up and turns to 45° to the right, the left foot takes a step back leftward, detach the feet for the shoulder–width apart. At the same time, cross the palms to lift overhead through the front of the chest, then part two palms to both sides, with the palms outward and the fingers up, keep the arms horizontal. Eyes look forward. (Figure 118)

七星螳螂拳 梅花路

圖 119

　　(2)上動不停。身體略向左轉，右腳向左腳前方上一步，腳跟著地，身體下蹲成七星步；同時，右掌下畫，經胸前向上、向外畫掌，掌心向前，掌指向上，高與肩平；左掌向裏畫掌，立掌於右肘內側下方，掌心向右，掌指向上；目視右掌。（圖 119）

梅花路套路動作圖解

(2) Keep the above action, the body turns to the left slightly, the right foot takes a step to the front of the left one with the heel on the ground. The body squats into the seven-star stance. At the same time, the right palm pall down, pull the palm upward and outward through the front of the chest, with the palm forward and the fingers up at the shoulder height; the left palm pulls inward under the inner side of the right elbow with the standing palm, with the palm rightward and the fingers up. Eyes look at the right palm. (Figure 119)

圖 120

52. 雙封閉門腳
Double wraps and close-up foot

(1)接上勢。右腳向前上半步,重心前移成右弓步;同時,兩掌在胸前畫一圓弧,再向前畫掌,兩掌心均向下,掌指均向前,略高於胯;目視兩掌。(圖120)

(1)Follow the above posture, the right foot takes a half-step forward, transfer the barycenter into the right bow stance. At the same time, the palms draw a circle before the chest, then pull the palms forward, with the palms down and the fingers forward, higher than the hip slightly. Eyes look at the palms. (Figure 120)

圖 121

(2)上動不停。身體略向左轉，重心後移至左腿；同時，兩掌變為螳螂鉤，向左、向後勾掛，鉤尖均向後，置於左胯側；目視右前方。（圖 121）

(2) Keep the above action, the body turns to the left slightly and transfer the barycenter back to the left leg. At the same time, change two palms into mantis hooks, hang leftward and backward, with the hook tips back ward and putting at the side of the left hip. Eyes look right forward.〔Figure 121〕

圖 122

（3）上動不停。左腿微屈獨立，右腿提起向上彈踢，腳面繃直，高與胯平；目視右腳。（圖 122）

（3）Keep the above action, bend the left leg slightly to stand alone, lift the right leg for snap kick upward, stretch the instep tight at the hip level. Eyes look at the right foot.（Figure 122）

圖 123

53. 螳螂雙封手　Mantis close-up hands

(1)接上勢。右腳向前落步，左轉身 90°，重心落於兩腿間；同時，右鉤手變掌，向右畫弧再向裏畫掌；左鉤手變掌外摟，兩掌交叉於腹前，掌心均向下；目視兩掌。（圖 123）

(1)Follow the above posture, the right foot falls forward, the body turns 90° to the left, with the barycenter between two legs. At the same time, change the right hook hand into palm, draw a curve rightward, then the palm pulls inward, change the left hook hand into palm for outward grab, cross the palms before the abdomen, with the palms down. Eyes look at the palms.
（Figure 123）

圖 124

（2）上動不停。身體略向後傾斜；同時，兩臂屈肘，兩掌在胸前翻轉絞手，右掌掌心向上，掌指向右；左掌心向右，兩掌高與頜平；目視前方。（圖124）

（2）Keep the above action, the body slants backward slightly. At the same time, bend elbows of two arms, turn over the palms to twist the hands before the chest, with the right palm up, the fingers rightward and the left palm rightward. Keep two palms high with the chin. Eyes look forward.（Figure 124）

圖 125

（3）上動不停。重心略前移；同時，右掌前探，掌心向前，虎口向上，高與肩平；左掌護於右肩前，掌指向上，掌心向外；目視右掌。（圖 125）

(3) Keep the above action, transfer the barycenter forward. At the same time, the right palm stretches forward, with the palm forward and tiger´s mouth up at the shoulder height; the left palm guards before the right shoulder, with the fingers up and the palm outward. Eyes look at the right palm.〔Figure 125〕

七星螳螂拳 梅花路

圖 126

⑷上動不停。右臂屈肘，右掌變為螳螂鉤，吊腕勾拉於胸前，鉤尖向下；同時，左掌向前探，掌心向外，掌指向前，高與肩平；目視左掌。（圖 126）

(4) Keep the above action, bend elbow of the right arm, change the palm into mantis hook, hang wrist and pull it before the chest, with the hook tip downward. At the same time, the left palm stretches forward, with the palm outward and the fingers forward at the shoulder height. Eyes look at the left palm. (Figure 126)

梅花路套路動作圖解

圖 127

(5)上動不停。身體下蹲;同時,左臂屈肘,左鉤
手吊腕回拉於左膝上方,略低於肩;目視左前方。
(圖 127)

(5) Keep the above action, the body squats down.At the
same time, bend elbow of the left arm, hang wrist of the left hook
hand to pull back above the left knee, lower than the shoulder.
Eyes look left forward.〔Figure 127〕

圖 128

54. 收勢　Closing form

(1)身體重心提起，略向右轉身；同時，兩鉤手變掌，經胸前上托，隨即向兩側分掌，兩臂成水平，兩掌心向外，掌指向上；目視右掌。（圖128）

(1) Lift the barycenter of the body and turn it to the right slightly. At the same time, change two hook hands into palms to lift through the front of the chest, then separate the palms to both sides. keep two arms horizontal, with the palms outward and the fingers up.Eyes look at the right palm.（Figure 128）

圖 129

　　⑵上動不停。左腳向右腳併步；同時，兩掌變拳抱於腰間；目視前方。（圖 129）

　　⑵ Keep the above action,bring the left foot and right one together. At the same time, change two palms into fists and hold on the waist. Eyes look forward.〔 Figure 129 〕

圖 130

（3）上動不停。兩拳變掌，自然下垂於身體兩側；目視前方。（圖 130）

要點：挺胸收腹，平心靜氣，體態自然，精神內斂。

(3) Keep the above action, change the fists into palms and drop on both side of the body naturally. Eyes look forward. 〔Figure 130〕

Key points: lift the chest, draw in the abdomen, Posture is natural and vital energy collects inward.

全套動作示意圖

Demonstration of All the Action

全套動作示意圖

圖 1

圖 2

圖 3

圖 4

圖 5

圖 6

圖 7

圖 8

圖 9

圖 9 附圖

七星螳螂拳 梅花路

图 14

图 13

图 12

图 11

图 10

图 19

图 18

图 17

图 16

图 15

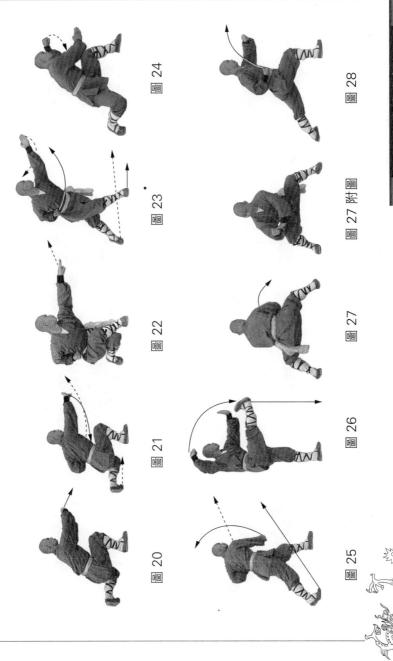

七星螳螂拳 梅花路

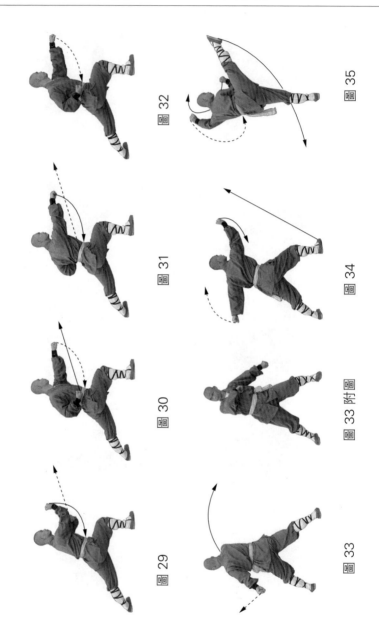

圖 35

圖 32

圖 34

圖 31

圖 33 附圖

圖 30

圖 33

圖 29

圖 38

圖 37 附圖

圖 37

圖 36 附圖

圖 36

圖 42

圖 41

圖 40

圖 39

七星螳螂拳　梅花路

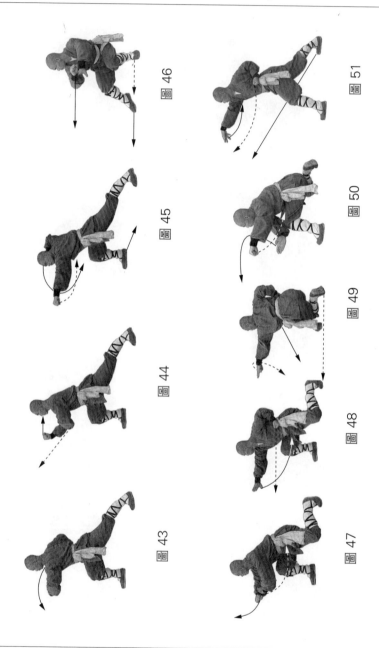

圖 46

圖 45

圖 44

圖 43

圖 51

圖 50

圖 49

圖 48

圖 47

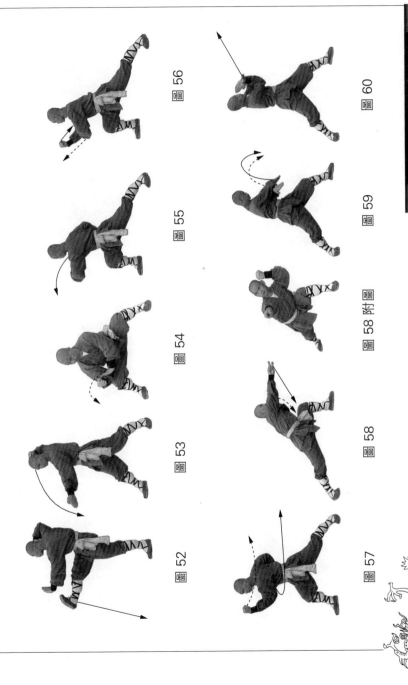

七星螳螂拳　梅花路

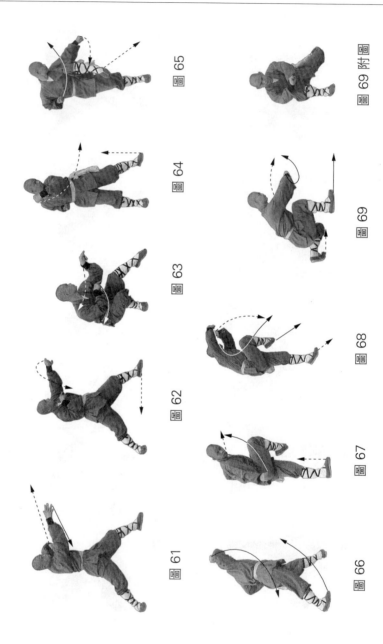

图 65

图附 69

图 64

图 69

图 63

图 68

图 62

图 67

图 61

图 66

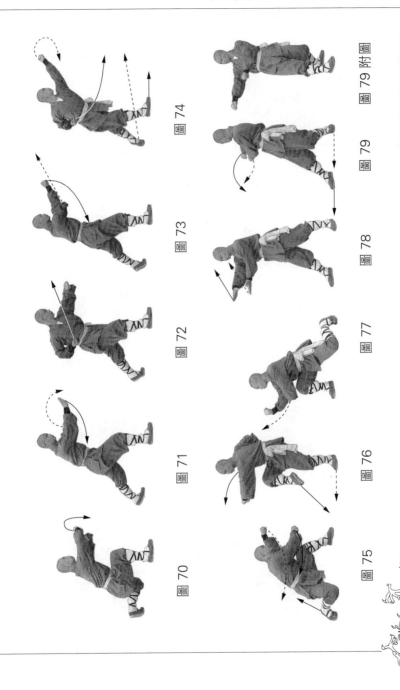

全套動作示意圖

圖70　圖71　圖72　圖73　圖74

圖75　圖76　圖77　圖78　圖79　圖79附

七星螳螂拳　梅花路

圖 83

圖 82

圖 81

圖 80

圖 88

圖 87

圖 86

圖 85

圖 84

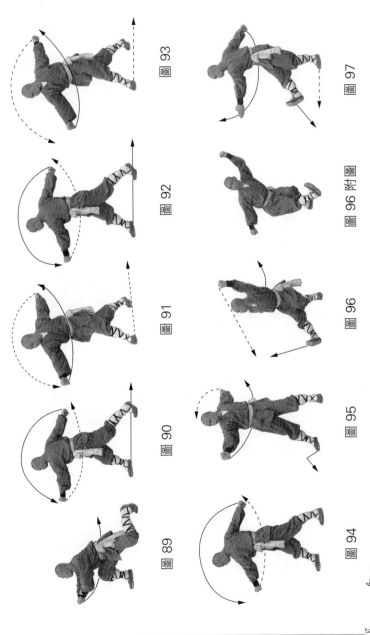

圖 93　　圖 92　　圖 91　　圖 90　　圖 89

圖 97　　圖 96 附圖　　圖 96　　圖 95　　圖 94

全套動作示意圖

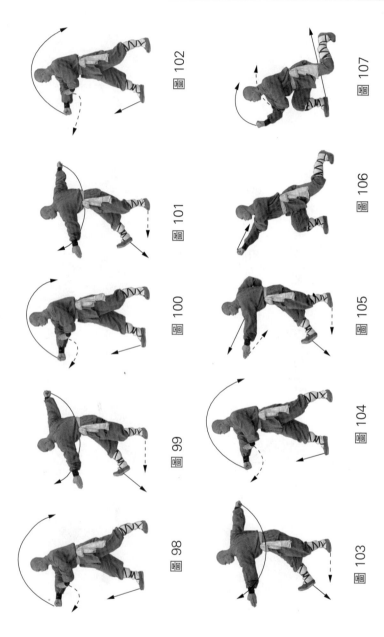

七星螳螂拳 梅花路

圖 102

圖 101

圖 100

圖 99

圖 98

圖 107

圖 106

圖 105

圖 104

圖 103

全套動作示意圖

圖 108　圖 109　圖 110　圖 111　圖 112

圖 113　圖 114　圖 115　圖 116　圖 117

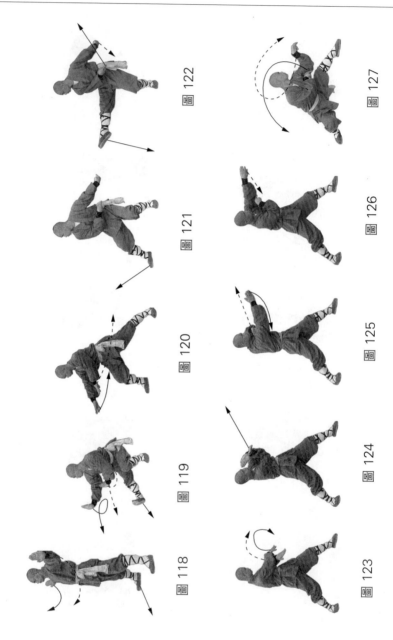

圖 122

圖 121

圖 120

圖 119

圖 118

圖 127

圖 126

圖 125

圖 124

圖 123

七星螳螂拳　梅花路

全套動作示意圖

圖 130

圖 129

圖 128

導引養生功 系列叢書

◎ 1. 疏筋壯骨功
◎ 2. 導引保健功
◎ 3. 頤身九段錦
◎ 4. 九九還童功
◎ 5. 舒心平血功
◎ 6. 益氣養肺功
◎ 7. 養生太極扇
◎ 8. 養生太極棒
◎ 9. 導引養生形體詩韻
◎ 10. 四十九式經絡動功

張廣德養生著作

每冊定價 350 元

全系列為彩色圖解附教學光碟

彩色圖解太極武術

1 太極功夫扇

定價220元

2 武當太極劍

定價220元

3 楊式太極劍

定價220元

4 楊式太極刀

定價220元

5 二十四式太極拳＋VCD

定價350元

6 三十二式太極劍＋VCD

定價350元

7 四十二式太極劍＋VCD

定價350元

8 四十二式太極拳＋VCD

定價350元

9 楊式十六式太極劍

定價350元

10 楊氏二十八式太極拳＋VCD

定價350元

11 楊式太極拳四十式＋VCD

定價350元

12 陳式太極拳五十六式＋VCD

定價350元

13 吳式太極拳五十六式＋VCD

定價350元

14 精簡陳式太極拳八式十六式

定價220元

15 精簡吳式太極拳三十六式拳架·推手

定價220元

16 夕陽美功夫扇

定價220元

17 綜合四十八式太極拳＋VCD

定價350元

18 三十二式太極拳 四段

定價220元

19 楊式三十七式太極拳＋VCD

定價350元

20 楊氏五十一式太極劍＋VCD
定價350元

養生保健

古今養生保健法 強身健體增加身體免疫力

1 醫療養生氣功
醫療養生氣功
定價250元

2 中國氣功圖譜
中國氣功圖譜
定價250元

3 少林醫療氣功精粹
少林醫療氣功精粹
定價250元

4 龍形實用氣功
龍形實用氣功
定價220元

5 魚戲增視強身氣功
魚戲增視強身氣功
定價220元

7 道家玄牝氣功
道家玄牝氣功
定價200元

8 仙家秘傳祛病功
仙家秘傳祛病功
定價160元

9 少林十大健身功
少林十大健身功
定價180元

10 中國自控氣功
中國自控氣功
定價250元

11 醫療防癌氣功
醫療防癌氣功
定價250元

12 醫療強身氣功
醫療強身氣功
定價250元

13 醫療點穴氣功
醫療點穴氣功
定價250元

14 中國八卦如意功
中國八卦如意功
定價180元

15 正宗馬禮堂養氣功
正宗馬禮堂養氣功
定價420元

16 秘傳道家筋經內丹功
秘傳道家筋經內丹功
定價300元

17 三元開慧功
三元開慧功
定價250元

18 防癌治癌新氣功
防癌治癌新氣功
定價180元

19 禪定與佛家氣功修煉
禪定與佛家氣功修煉
定價200元

20 顛倒之術
顛倒之術
定價360元

21 簡明氣功辭典
簡明氣功辭典
定價360元

22 八卦三合功
八卦三合功
定價230元

23 朱砂掌健身養生功
朱砂掌健身養生功
定價250元

24 抗老功
抗老功
定價230元

25 意氣按穴排濁自療法
意氣按穴排濁自療法
定價250元

27 健身祛病小功法
健身祛病小功法
定價200元

28 張氏太極混元功
張氏太極混元功
定價250元

29 中國璇密功
中國璇密功
定價250元

30 中國少林禪密功
中國少林禪密功
定價200元

31 郭林新氣功
郭林新氣功
定價400元

32 八卦之源與健身養生
定價280元

33 現代原始氣功1
現代原始氣功1
定價400元

34 養生開脈太極
養生開脈太極
定價300元

太極跤

1 太極防身術
定價300元

2 擒拿術
定價280元

3 中國式摔角
定價350元

簡化太極拳

1 陳式太極拳十三式
定價200元

2 楊式太極拳十三式
定價200元

3 吳式太極拳十三式
定價200元

4 武式太極拳十三式
定價200元

5 孫式太極拳十三式
定價200元

6 趙堡太極拳十三式
定價200元

原地太極拳

1 原地綜合太極拳二十四式
定價220元

2 原地活步太極拳四十二式
定價200元

3 原地簡化太極拳二十四式
定價200元

4 原地太極拳十二式
定價200元

5 原地青少年太極拳二十二式
定價220元

6 原地兒童太極拳十捶十六式
定價180元

健康加油站

1 糖尿病預防與治療
定價200元

2 胃部機能與強健
定價180元

3 不孕症治療
定價200元

4 簡易醫學急救法
定價200元

5 肥胖健康診療
定價200元

6 肝功能健康診療
定價200元

7 高血壓健康診療
定價200元

8 高血糖值健康診療
定價200元

9 尿酸值健康診療
定價200元

10 膽固醇中性脂肪健康診療
定價200元

11 痛風劇痛消除法
定價180元

12 三溫暖健康法
定價180元

13 手・腳病理按摩
定價180元

14 B型肝炎預防與治療
定價180元

15 吃得更漂亮健康
定價180元

16 茶使您更健康
定價180元

17 圖解常見疾病運動療法
定價180元

18 科學健身改變亞健康
定價180元

19 簡易萬病自療保健
定價220元

20 王朝秘藥媚酒
定價180元

運動精進叢書

1 怎樣跑得快

定價200元

2 怎樣投得遠

定價180元

3 怎樣跳得遠

定價180元

4 怎樣跳的高

定價180元

5 高爾夫揮桿原理

定價220元

6 網球技巧圖解

定價220元

7 排球技巧圖解

定價230元

8 沙灘排球技巧圖解

定價230元

9 撞球技巧圖解

定價230元

10 籃球技巧圖解

定價220元

11 足球技巧圖解

定價230元

12 羽毛球技巧圖解

定價220元

13 乒乓球技巧圖解

定價220元

14 曲線球與飛碟球

定價300元

15 街頭花式籃球

定價280元

16 精彩高爾夫

定價330元

17 巴西青少年足球訓練方法

定價230元

快樂健美站

1
柔力健身球

定價280元

2
自行車健康享瘦

定價280元

3
跑步鍛鍊走路減肥

定價280元

4
創造健康的肌力訓練

定價220元

5
舒適超級伸展體操

定價280元

6
水中有氧運動

定價280元

7
雕塑完美身材

定價280元

8
創造超級兒童

定價280元

9
使頭腦變聰明

定價280元

10
防止老化的身體改造訓練

定價280元

11
三個月塑身計畫

定價280元

12
懶人族瑜伽

定價280元

13
忙裡偷閒練瑜伽基礎篇

定價240元

14
忙裡偷閒練瑜伽祛病養生篇

定價240元

15
健身跑激發身體的潛能

定價200元

16
中華鐵球健身操

定價180元

17
彼拉提斯健身寶典

定價280元

18
全身保健操＋VCD

定價280元

19
瑜伽美姿美容

定價180元

20
豐胸做自信女人

定價200元

21
輕鬆瑜伽治百病

定價280元

常見病藥膳調養叢書

1 脂肪肝四季飲食
定價200元

2 高血壓四季飲食
定價200元

3 慢性腎炎四季飲食
定價200元

4 高脂血症四季飲食
定價200元

5 慢性胃炎四季飲食
定價200元

6 糖尿病四季飲食
定價200元

7 癌症四季飲食
定價200元

8 痛風四季飲食
定價200元

9 肝炎四季飲食
定價200元

10 肥胖症四季飲食
定價200元

11 膽囊炎、膽石症四季飲食
定價200元

傳統民俗療法

1 神奇刀療法
定價200元

2 神奇拍打療法
定價200元

3 神奇拔罐療法
定價200元

4 神奇艾灸療法
定價200元

5 神奇貼敷療法
定價200元

6 神奇薰洗療法
定價200元

7 神奇耳穴療法
定價200元

8 神奇指針療法
定價200元

9 神奇藥酒療法
定價200元

10 神奇藥茶療法
定價200元

11 神奇推拿療法
定價200元

12 神奇止痛療法
定價200元

13 神奇天然藥食物療法
定價200元

14 神奇新穴療法
定價200元

15 神奇小針刀療法
定價200元

16 神奇刮痧療法
定價200元

品冠文化出版社

國家圖書館出版品預行編目資料

七星螳螂拳　梅花路／耿　軍　趙會斌　著
　　──初版，──臺北市，大展，2007〔民96〕
　　面；21公分，──（少林傳統功夫漢英對照系列；5）
　　ISBN　978-957-468-545-5（平裝）

　1.拳術－中國

528.97　　　　　　　　　　　　　　　　96008339

七星螳螂拳　梅花路　　ISBN　978-957-468-545-5

著　　　者／耿　軍　趙會斌
責任編輯／張建林
發 行 人／蔡森明
出 版 者／大展出版社有限公司
社　　　址／台北市北投區（石牌）致遠一路2段12巷1號
電　　　話／（02）28236031・28236033・28233123
傳　　　眞／（02）28272069
郵政劃撥／01669551
網　　　址／www.dah-jaan.com.tw
E－mail／service@dah-jaan.com.tw
登 記 證／局版臺業字第2171號
承 印 者／高星印刷品行
裝　　　訂／建鑫裝訂有限公司
排 版 者／弘益電腦排版有限公司
授 權 者／北京人民體育出版社
初版1刷／2007年（民96年）7月

定　價／200元

大展好書　好書大展
品嘗好書　冠群可期

大展好書　好書大展

品嘗好書　冠群可期